I0118802

John G. Bourke

Compilation of Notes and Memoranda

bearing upon the use of human ordure and human urine in rites of a religious or semi-religious character among various nations

John G. Bourke

Compilation of Notes and Memoranda
bearing upon the use of human ordure and human urine in rites of a religious or semi-religious character among various nations

ISBN/EAN: 9783337262709

Printed in Europe, USA, Canada, Australia, Japan

Cover: Foto ©Andreas Hilbeck / pixelio.de

More available books at **www.hansebooks.com**

OF

NOTES AND MEMORANDA

BEARING UPON THE USE OF

HUMAN ORDURE AND HUMAN URINE

IN

RITES OF A RELIGIOUS OR SEMI-RELIGIOUS CHARACTER

AMONG

VARIOUS NATIONS.

BY

JOHN G. BOURKE, Captain, Third Cavalry, United States Army.

FELLOW OF THE AMERICAN ASSOCIATION FOR THE ADVANCEMENT OF SCIENCE; MEMBER OF THE ANTHROPOLOGICAL SOCIETY OF WASHINGTON, D. C.; AUTHOR OF THE "SNAKE DANCE OF THE MOQUIS OF ARIZONA," "AN APACHE CAMPAIGN," ETC.

WASHINGTON, D. C.:
1888.

CONTENTS.

URINE DANCES AND UR-ORGIES.

The object of the present monograph is to arrange in a form for easy reference such allusions as have come under the author's notice bearing upon the use of human ordure, or urine, or articles apparently intended as substitutes for them, whether in rites of a clearly religious or "medicine" type or in those which, while not pronouncedly such, have about them suggestions that they may be survivals of a former existence of urine dances or ur-orgies among tribes and peoples from whose later mode of life and thought they have been eliminated.

The difficulties surrounding the elucidation of this topic will, no doubt, occur at once to every student of anthropology or ethnology. The rites and practices herein spoken of are to be found only in communities isolated from the world, and are such as even savages would shrink from revealing unnecessarily to strangers; while, too frequently, observers of intelligence have failed to improve opportunities for noting the existence of rites of this nature, or else, restrained by a false modesty, have clothed their remarks in vague and indefinite phraseology, forgetting that as a physician, to be skillful, must study his patients both in sickness and in health, so the anthropologist must study man, not alone wherein he reflects the grandeur of his Maker, but likewise in his grosser and more animal propensities.

Repugnant, therefore, as the subject is under most points of view, the author has felt constrained to reproduce all that he has seen and read, hoping that in the fuller consideration which all forms of primitive religion are now receiving this, the most brutal, possibly, of them all, may claim some share of examination and discussion.

To serve as a nucleus for notes and memoranda since gleaned, the author has reproduced his original monograph, first published in the Transactions of the American Association for the Advancement of Science, 1885, and read by title at the Ann Arbor, Michigan, meeting, in the same year.

The Urine Dance of the Zunis.

On the evening of November 17, 1881, during my stay in the village of Zuni, New Mexico, the *Nehue-Cue*, one of the secret orders of the Zunis, sent word to Mr. Frank H. Cushing* (whose guest I was) that they would do us the unusual honor of coming to our house to give us one of their characteristic dances, which, Cushing said, was unprecedented.

The squaws of the governor's family put the long "living room" to rights, sweeping the floor and sprinkling it with water to lay the dust. Soon after dark the dancers entered; they were twelve in number, two being boys. The center men were naked with the exception of black breech-clouts of archaic style. The hair was worn naturally, with a bunch of wild turkey feathers tied in front and one of corn-husks over each ear. White bands were painted across the face at eyes and mouth. Each wore a collar or neckcloth of black woolen stuff. Broad white bands, one inch wide, were painted around the body at the navel, around the arms, the legs at mid thighs and knees. Tortoise-shell rattles hung from the right knee. Blue woolen footless leggins were worn with low-cut moccasins, and in the right hand each waved a wand made of an ear of corn, trimmed with the plumage of the wild turkey and macaw. The others were arrayed in old cast-off American Army clothing, and all wore white cotton night-caps, with corn-husks twisted into the hair at top of head and ears. Several wore, in addition to the tortoise-shell rattles, strings of brass sleigh-bells at knees. One was more grotesquely attired than the rest in a long India-rubber gossamer "overall" and a pair of goggles, painted white, over his eyes. His general "get-up" was a spirited take-off upon a Mexican priest. Another was a very good counterfeit of a young woman.

To the accompaniment of an oblong drum and of the rattles and bells spoken of they shuffled into the long room, crammed with spectators of both sexes and of all sizes and ages. Their song was apparently a ludicrous reference to everything and everybody in sight, Cushing, Mindeleff, and myself receiving special attention, to the uncontrolled merriment of the red-skinned listeners. I had taken my station at one side of the room, seated upon the banquette, and having in front of me a rude bench or table, upon which was a small coal-oil lamp. I suppose that in the halo diffused by the feeble light and in my "stained-glass attitude" I must have borne some resemblance to the pictures of saints hanging upon the walls of old Mexican churches; to such a fancied resemblance I at least attribute the performance which followed.

The dancers suddenly wheeled into line, threw themselves on their knees before my table, and with extravagant beatings of breast began an outlandish but faithful mockery of a Mexican Catholic congregation at vespers. One bawled out a parody upon the Paternoster, another mumbled along in the manner of an old man reciting the rosary, while the fellow with the India-rubber coat jumped up and began a passionate exhortation or sermon, which for mimetic fidelity was incomparable. This kept the audience laughing with sore sides for some moments, until at a signal from the leader the dancers suddenly countermarched out of the room, in single file, as they had entered.

An interlude followed of ten minutes, during which the dusty floor was sprinkled by men who spat water forcibly from their mouths. The *Nehue-Cue* re-entered; this time two of their number were stark naked. Their singing was very peculiar and sounded like a chorus of chimney-sweeps, and their dance became a stiff-legged jump, with heels kept twelve inches apart. After they had ambled around the room two or three times, Cushing announced in the Zuni language that a "feast" was ready for them, at which

---

* Mr. Cushing's reputation as an ethnologist is now so firmly established in two continents that no reference to his self-sacrificing and invaluable labors in the cause of science seems to be necessary.

they loudly roared their approbation and advanced to strike hands with the munificent "Americanos," addressing us in a funny gibberish of broken Spanish, English, and Zuni. They then squatted upon the ground and consumed with zest large "ollas" full of tea, and dishes of hard tack and sugar. As they were about finishing this a squaw entered, carrying an "olla" of urine, of which the filthy brutes drank heartily.

I refused to believe the evidence of my senses, and asked Cushing if that were really human urine. "Why, certainly," replied he, "and here comes more of it." This time, it was a large tin pailful, not less than two gallons. I was standing by the squaw as she offered this strange and abominable refreshment. She made a motion with her hand to indicate to me that it was urine, and one of the old men repeated the Spanish word *mear* (to urinate), while my sense of smell demonstrated the truth of their statements.

The dancers swallowed great draughts, smacked their lips, and, amid the roaring merriment of the spectators, remarked that it was very, very good. The clowns were now upon their mettle, each trying to surpass his neighbors in feats of nastiness. One swallowed a fragment of corn-husk, saying he thought it very good and better than bread; his *vis-à-vis* attempted to chew and gulp down a piece of filthy rag. Another expressed regret that the dance had not been held out of doors, in one of the plazas; there they could show what they could do. There they always made it a point of honor to eat the excrement of men and dogs.

For my own part I felt satisfied with the omission, particularly as the room, stuffed with one hundred Zunis, had become so foul and filthy as to be almost unbearable. The dance, as good luck would have it, did not last many minutes, and we soon had a chance to run into the refreshing night air.

To this outline description of a disgusting rite I have little to add. The Zunis, in explanation, stated that the *Nehue-Cue* were a Medicine Order which held these dances from time to time to inure the stomachs of members to any kind of food, no matter how revolting. This statement may seem plausible enough when we understand that religion and medicine among primitive races are almost always one and the same thing, or, at least, so closely intertwined that it is a matter of difficulty to decide where one begins and the other ends.

Religion in its dramatic ceremonial preserves, to some extent, the history of the particular race in which it dwells. Among nations of high development, miracles, moralities, and passion plays have taught, down to our own day, in object lessons, the sacred history in which the spectators believed. Some analogous purpose may have been held in view by the first organizers of the urine dance. In their early history, the Zunis and other Pueblos suffered from constant warfare with savage antagonists and with each other. From the position of their villages, long sieges must of necessity have been sustained, in which sieges famine and disease, no doubt, were the allies counted upon by the investing forces. We may have in this abominable dance a tradition of the extremity to which the Zunis of the long ago were reduced at some unknown period. A similar catastrophe in the history of the Jews is intimated in II Kings, xviii, 27; and again in Isaiah, xxxvi, 12: "But Rab-shakeh said unto them: hath my master sent me to thy master, and to thee to speak these words? hath he not sent me to the men which sit on the wall, that they may *eat their own dung and drink their own piss* with you?" In the course of my studies I came across a reference to a very similar dance, occurring among one of the fanatical sects of the Arabian Bedouins, but the journal in which it was recorded, the *London Lancet*, I think, was unfortunately mislaid.

As illustrative of the tenacity with which such vile ceremonial, once adopted by a sect, will adhere to it and become ingrafted upon its life, long after the motives which have suggested or commended it have vanished in oblivion, let me quote a few lines from Max Müller's "Chips from a German Workshop," "Essay upon the Parsees," pp. 163, 164,

Scribner's edition, 1869: "The *nirang* is the urine of a cow, ox, or she-goat, and the rubbing of it over the face and hands is the second thing a Parsee does after getting out of bed. Either before applying the *nirang* to the face and hands, or while it remains on the hands after being applied, he should not touch anything directly with his hands; but, in order to wash out the *Nirang*, he either asks somebody else to pour water on his hands, or resorts to the device of taking hold of the pot through the intervention of a piece of cloth, such as a handkerchief, or his *sudra*, *i. e.*, his blouse. He first pours water on his hand, then takes the pot in that hand and washes his other hand, face, and feet." (Quoting from *Dadabhai-Nadrosi's* Description of the Parsees.)

Continuing, Max Muller says: "Strange as this process of purification may appear, it becomes perfectly disgusting when we are told that women, after childbirth, have not only to undergo this sacred ablution, but actually to drink a little of the *nirang*, and that the same rite is imposed on children at the time of their investiture with the *Sudra* and *Koshti*, the badges of the Zoroastrian faith."

THE FEAST OF FOOLS IN EUROPE.

Closely corresponding to this urine dance of the Zunis was the Feast of Fools, in Continental Europe, the description of which, here given, is quoted from Dulaure:

La grand'messe commençait alors; tous les ecclésiastiques y assistaient, le visage barbouillé de noir, ou convert d'un masque hideux ou ridicule. Pendant la célébration, les uns, vêtus en baladins ou en femmes, dansaient au milieu du chœur et y chantaient des chansons bouffones ou obscènes. Les autres venaient manger sur l'autel des saucisses et des boudins, jouer aux cartes ou aux dez, devant le prêtre célébrant, l'encensaient avec un encensoir, ou brûlaient de vieilles savates, et lui en faisaient respirer la fumée.

Après la messe, nouveaux actes d'extravagance et d'impiété. Les prêtres, confondus avec les habitans des deux sexes, couraient, dansaient dans l'église, s'excitaient à toutes les folies, à toutes les actions licencieuses que leur inspirait une imagination effrénée. Plus de honte, plus de pudeur; aucune digue n'arrêtait le débordement de la folie et des passions. * * * * *

Au milieu du tumulte, des blasphêmes et des chants dissolus, on voyait les uns se dépouiller entièrement de leurs habits, d'autres se livrer aux actes du plus honteux libertinage.

* * * Les acteurs, montés sur des tombereaux pleins d'ordures, s'amusaient à en jeter à la populace qui les entouraient. * * * Ces scènes étaient toujours accompagnées de chansons ordurières et impies.—(Dulaure, "Des Divinités Génératrices," chap. xv, p. 315, et seq., Paris, 1825.)

COMPARISON BETWEEN THE FEAST OF FOOLS AND THE URINE DANCE.

In the above description may be seen that the principal actors (taking possession of the church during high mass) had their faces daubed and painted, or masked in a harlequin manner; that they were dressed as clowns or as women; that they ate upon the altar itself sausages and blood-puddings. Now the word blood-pudding, in French, is *boudin*—but *boudin* also meant *excrement.** Add to this the feature that these

*See in Dictionary of French and English Language, by Ferdinand E. A. Gasc, London, Bell and Daldy, York street, Covent Garden, 1873.

Littré, whose work appeared in 1863, gives as one of his definitions, "anything that is shaped like a sausage."

Bescherelle, Spiers and Surenne and Boyer, do not give Gasc's definition.

clowns, after leaving the church, took their stand in dung-carts (*tomber-eaux*), and threw *ordure* upon the bystanders; and finally that some of these actors appeared perfectly naked ("on voyait les ùns se dépouiller entièrement de leurs habits"), and it must be admitted that there is certainly a wonderful concatenation of resemblances between these filthy and inexplicable rites on different sides of a great ocean.

THE FEAST OF FOOLS TRACED BACK TO MOST ANCIENT TIMES.

Dulaure makes no attempt to trace the origin of these ceremonies in France; he contents himself with saying, "ces cérémonies * * * ont subsisté pendant douze ou quinze siècles," or, in other words, that they were of Pagan origin. In twelve or fifteen hundred years the rite might well have been sublimed from the eating of pure excrement, as among the Zunis, to the consumption of the "*boudin*," the excrement symbol.* Conceding for the moment that this suspicion is correct, we have a proof of the antiquity of the urine dance among the Zunis. So great is the resemblance between the Zuni rite and that just described by Dulaure, that we should have reason for believing that the new country borrowed from the old some of the features transmitted to the present day, and were there not evidence of a wider distribution of this observance, it might be assumed that the Catholic missionaries (who worked among the Zunis from 1580, or thereabout, and excepting during intervals of revolt remained on duty in Zuni down to the period of American occupation) found the obscene and disgusting orgie in full vigor, and realizing the danger, by unwise precipitancy, of destroying all hopes of winning over this people, shrewdly concluded to tacitly accept the religious abnormality and to engraft upon it the plant flourishing so bravely in the vicinity of their European homes.

DISAPPEARANCE OF THE FEAST OF FOOLS.

In France, the Feast of Fools disappeared only with the French Revolution; in other parts of Continental Europe it began to wane about the time of the Reformation. In England, "the abbot of unreason," whose pranks are outlined by Sir Walter Scott, in his novel, "The Abbot," the miracle plays which had once served a good purpose in teaching scriptural lessons to an illiterate peasantry, and the "moralities" of same general purport, faded away under the stern antagonism of the Puritan

* And very probably a phallic symbol also.

iconoclast. The Feast of Fools, as such, was abolished by Henry VIII A. D. 1541. (See "The English Reformation," Francis Charles Massingberd, London, 1857, p. 125.*) Picart's account of the Feast of Fools is similar to that given by Dulaure. He says that it took place in the church, at Christmas tide, and was borrowed from the Roman Saturnalia; was never approved of by the Christian church, as a body, but fought against from the earliest times:

> Les uns étoient masqués ou avec des visages barbouillés qui faisoïent peur ou qui faisoïent rire; les autres en habits de femmes ou de pantomimes, tels que sont les ministres du théâtre.
>
> Ils dansoient dans le choeur, en entrant, et chantoient, des chansons obscènes. Les Diacres et les sou-diacres prenoient plaisir à mager des boudins et des saucisses sur l'autel, au nez du prêtre célébrant; ils jouoient à des seux aux cartes et aux dés; ils mettoient dans l'encensoir quelques morceaux de vieilles savates pour lui faire respirer une mauvaise odeur.
>
> Après la messe, chacun couroit, sautoit et dansoit par l'église avec tant d'impudence, que quelques uns n'àvoient pas honte de se porter à toutes sortes d'indécences et de se dépouiller entièremênt; ensuite, ils se faisoïent trainer par les rues dans des tombereaux pleins d'ordures, d'ou ils prenoient plaisir d'en jeter à la populace qui s'assembloit autour d'eux.
>
> Ils s'arrétoient et faisoient de leurs corps des mouvements et des postures lascives qu'ils accompagnoient de paroles impudiques.
>
> Les plus impudiques d'entre les seculiers se mêloient parmi le clergé, pour faire aussi quelques personnages de Foux en habits ecclésiastiques de Moines et de Religieuses.—(Picart, "Coûtumes et Cérémonies réligieuses de toutes les Nations du Monde," Amsterdam, Holland, 1729, vol. ix, pp. 5, 6.)

Diderot and d'Alembert use almost the same terms; the officiating clergy were clad "les uns comme des bouffons, les autres en habits de femmes ou masqués d'une façon monstrueuse * * * ils mangeaient et jouaient aux dés sur l'autel à côté du prêtre qui célébroit la messe. Ils mettoient des ordures dans les encensoirs." They say that the details would not bear repetition. This feast prevailed generally in Continental Europe from Christmas to Epiphany, and in England, especially in York. (Diderot and d'Alembert, Encyclopædia, "Fete des Fous," Geneva, Switzerland, 1779.)

THE COMMEMORATIVE CHARACTER OF RELIGIOUS FESTIVALS.

The opinion expressed above concerning the commemorative character of religious festivals echoes that which Godfrey Higgins ennunciated sev-

---

*Faber advances the opinion that the "mummers" or clowns who figured in the pastimes of the abbot of unreason, &c., bear a strong resemblance to the animal-headed Egyptian priests in the sacred dances represented on the Bembine or Isiac table. (See Faber's "Pagan Idolatry," London, 1816, vol. 2, p. 479.)

ral generations ago. The learned author of Anacalypsis says that fesivals, "accompanied with dancing and music, * * were established to :eep in recollection victories or other important events." (Higgins' \nacalypsis, London, 1810, vol. 2, p. 424.) He argues the subject at ome length on pages 424–426, but the above is sufficient for the present)urpose.

In the religious rites of a people I should expect to find the earliest of their habits and ustoms.—(Higgins' Anacalypsis, vol. 1, p. 15.)

Applying the above remark to the Zuni dance, it may be interpreted is a dramatic pictograph of some half-forgotten episode in tribal history. Co strengthen this view by example, let us recall the fact that the Army)f Crusaders under Peter the Hermit* was so closely beleagured by the Moslems in Nicomedia in Bithynia that they were compelled to drink :heir own urine.† We read the narrative set out in cold type. The Zunis would have transmitted a record of the event by a dramatic rep·esentation which time would incrust with all the veneration that religion :ould impart.

Dancing was originally merely religious, intended to assist the memory in retaining the acred learning which originated previous to the invention of letters.

Indeed, I believe that there were no part of the rites and ceremonies of antiquity which vere not adopted with a view to keep in recollection the ancient learning before letters vere known.—(Higgins' Anacalypsis, vol. 2. p. 179.)

FRAY DIEGO DURAN'S ACCOUNT OF THE MEXICAN FESTIVALS.

All that Higgins believed was believed and asserted by the Dominican missionary Diego Duran. Duran complains bitterly that the unwise destruction of the ancient Mexican pictographs and all that explained the religion of the natives left the missionaries in ignorance as to what was religion and what was not. The Indians, taking advantage of this, mocked and ridiculed the dogmas and ceremonies of the new creed in the very face of its expounders, who still lacked a complete mastery of the language of the conquered. The Indians never could be induced to admit that they still adhered to their old superstitions, or that they were boldly indulging in their religious observances; many times, says the shrewd old chronicler, it would appear that they were merely indulging in some pleasant pastime, while they were really engaged in idolatry; or that

* Purchas. Pilgrims, lib. 8, chap. 1, p. 1191, London, 1622. Neither Gibbon nor Michaud expresses this fact so clearly, but each speaks of the terrible sufferings which decimated the undisciplined hordes of Peter and Walter the Penniless, and reduced the survivors to cannibalism.

† In one of the sieges of Samaria it is recorded that "the fourth part of a cab of dove's dung sold for five pieces of silver." (2 Kings, vi: 25.)

they were playing games, when truly they were casting lots for future events before the priest's eyes; or that they were subjecting themselves to penitential discipline, when they were sacrificing to their gods. This remark applied to all that they did. In dances, in baths, in markets, in singing their songs, in their dramas (the word is "*comedia*," a comedy, but a note in the margin of the manuscript says that probably this ought to be "*comida*," food, or dinner, or feast), in sowing, in reaping, in putting away the harvest in their granaries, even in tilling the ground, in building their houses, in their funerals, in their burials, in marriages, in the birth of children, into everything they did entered idolatry and superstition.

Parece muchas veces pensar que estan haciendo placer y estan idolatrando; y pensar que estan jugando y estan echando suertes de los sucesos delante de nuestros ojos y no los entendemos y pensamos que se disciplinan y estanse sacrificando.

Y asi erraron mucho los que con bueno celo (pero no con mucha prudencia), quemaron y destruyeron al principio todas las pinturas de antiguallas que tenian; pues, nos dejaron tan sin luz que delante de nuestros ojos idolatran y no los entendemos.

En los mitotes, en los baños, en los mercados, y en los cantares que cantan lamentando sus Dioses y sus Señores Antiguos, en las comedias, en los banquetes, y en el diferenciar en el de ellas, en todo se halla supersticion é idolátria; en el sembrar, en el coger, en el encerrar en los troges, hasta en el labrar la tierra y edificar las casas; pues en los mortuorios y entierros, y en los casamientos y en los nacimientos de los niños, especialmente si era hijo de algun Señor, eran estrañas las ceremonias que se le hacian; y donde todo se perfeccionaba era en la celebracion de las fiestas; finalmente, en todo mezclaban superSticion é idolatria; hasta en irse á bañarse al rio los viejos, puesto escrúpulo á la republica sino fuese habiendo precedido tales y tales ceremonias; todo lo cual nos es encubierto por el gran secreto que tienen.—(Diego Duran, lib. 2, concluding remarks.)

Fray Diego Duran, a Fray Predicador of the Dominican Order, says, at the end of his second volume, that it was finished in 1581.

The very same views were held by Father Geronimo Boscána, a Franciscan, who ministered for seventeen years to the Indians of California. Every act of an Indian's life was guided by religion. (See "Chinigchinich," included in A. A. Robinson's "California," New York, 1850.)

The Apaches have dances in which the prehistoric condition of the tribe is thus represented; so have the Mojaves and the Zunis; while in the snake dance of the Moquis and the sun dance of the Sioux the same faithful adherence to traditional costume and manners is apparent.

THE URINE DANCE OF THE ZUNIS MAY CONSERVE A TRADITION OF THE TIME WHEN VILE ALIMENT WAS IN USE.

The Zuni urine dance may therefore not improperly be considered, among other points of view, under that which suggests a commemoration of the earliest life of this people, when vile aliment of every kind may have been in use through necessity.

An examination of evidence will show that foods now justly regarded as noxious were once not unknown to nations of even greater development than any as yet attained by the Rio Grande Pueblos. Necessity was not always the inciting motive; frequently religious frenzy was responsible for orgies of which only vague accounts and still vaguer explanations have come down to us.

EXCREMENT USED IN HUMAN FOOD.

The very earliest accounts of the Indians of Florida and Texas refer to the use of such aliment. Cabeça de Vaca, one of the survivors of the ill-fated expedition of Panfilo de Narvaez, was a prisoner among various tribes for many years, and finally, accompanied by three comrades as wretched as himself, succeeded in traversing the continent, coming out at Culiacan, on the Pacific coast, in 1536.

His narrative says that the "Floridians" for food dug roots, and that they ate spiders, ant's eggs, worms, lizards, salamanders, snakes, earth, wood, the dung of deer, and many other things."* The same account, given in Purchas' Pilgrims (vol. 4, lib. 8, cap. 1, sec. 2, p. 1512), expresses it that "they also eat earth, wood, and whatever they can get; the dung of wild beasts." These remarks may be understood as applying to all tribes seen by this early explorer east of the Rocky Mountains.

Gómara identifies this loathsome diet with a particular tribe, the "Yaguaces" of Florida. "They eat spiders, ants, worms, lizards of two kinds, snakes, wood, earth, and ordure of all kinds of wild animals."†

The California Indians were still viler. The German Jesuit, Father Jacob Baegert, speaking of the Lower Californians (among whom he resided continuously from 1748 to 1765), says:

> They eat the seeds of the pitahaya [giant cactus] which have passed off undigested from their own stomachs; they gather their own excrement, separate the seeds from it, roast, grind, and eat them, making merry over the loathsome meal.

---

*Ils mangent des araignées, des œufs de fourmis, des vers, des lézards, des salamandres, des couleuvres, de la terre, du bois, de la fiente de cerfs et bien d'autres choses.—(Alvar Nuñez Cabeça de Vaca, in Ternaux, vol 7, p. 144.)

†Comen arañas, hormigas, gusanos, salamanquesas, lagartijas, culebras, palos, tierra y cagajones y cagurratas. (Gómara "Historia de las Indias," p. 182.) He derives his information from the narrative of Vaca. The word "cagajon" means horse dung, the dung of mules and asses; "cagarruta" the dung of sheep, goats, and mice.

And again:

In the mission of St. Ignatius * * * there are persons who will attach a piece of meat to a string and swallow it and pull it out again a dozen times in succession for the sake of protracting the enjoyment of its taste.—(Translation of Dr. Charles F. Rau, in Annual Report Smithsonian Institution, 1866, p. 363.)

A similar use of meat tied to a string is understood to have once been practiced by European sailors for the purpose of teasing green comrades suffering from the agonies of sea-sickness.

Castañeda alludes to the Californians as a race of naked savages who ate their own excrement.*

The same information is to found in Clavigero ("Historia de la Baja California," Mexico, 1852, p. 24), and in H. H. Bancroft's "Native Races of the Pacific Slope," vol. 1, p. 561, both of whom derive from Father Baegert. Orozco y Berra also has the story, but he adds that oftentimes numbers of the Californians would meet and pass the delicious titbit from mouth to mouth.†

The Indians of British North America, according to Harmon, "boil the buffalo paunch, with much of its dung adhering to it"—a filthy mode of cooking, which in itself would mean little since it can be paralleled in almost all tribes; but, in another paragraph, the same author says, "many consider a broth made by means of the dung of the cariboo and the hare to be a dainty dish." (Harmon's Journal, &c., Andover, 1820, p. 324.‡)

The Abbé Domenech asserts the same of the bands near Lake Superior:

In boiling their wild rice to eat they mix it with the excrement of rabbit—a delicacy appreciated by the epicures among them.—(Domenech. "Deserts," vol. 2, p. 311.)

Of the negroes of Guinea, an old authority relates that they "ate filthy, stinking elephant's and buffalo's flesh, wherein there is a thousand maggots, and many times stinks like carrion. * * * They eat

*Peuplé de sauvages qui vont tous nus et qui mangent leurs propres ordures.—(Castañeda, Ternaux, vol. 9, p. 156.)

Castañeda de Nagera accompanied the expedition of Francisco Vasquez de Coronado which entered Arizona, New Mexico, and the buffalo country in 1540–'42. Part of this expedition, under Don Garcia Lope de Cardena, went down the Colorado River, which separates California from Arizona, while another detachment, under Melchior Diaz, struck the river closer to its mouth and crossed into California.

†Algunas veces se juntan varios Indios y á la redonda va corriendo el bocado de uno en otro.—(Orozco y Berra, "Geografia de las lenguas de Mejico," Mexico, 1854, p. 359.)

‡Harmon's notes are of special interest at this point, because he is speaking of the Ta-cully or Carriers, who belong to the same Tinneh stock as the Apaches and Navajoes of Arizona and New Mexico, Lipans of Texas, Umpquas of Washington Territory, Hoopahs of California, and Slow-cuss of the head-waters of the Columbia River.

raw dogge guts, and never seethe nor roast them."* And another says that the Mossagueyes make themselves "a pottage with milk and fresh dung of kine, which, mixed together and heat at the fire, they drinke saying it makes them strong." (Purchas, lib. 9, cap. 12, sec. 4, p. 1555.)

The Peruvians ate their meat and fish raw, but nothing further is said by Gómara.†

HUMAN ORDURE EATEN BY EAST INDIAN FANATICS.

Speaking of the remnants of the Hindu sect of the Aghozis, an English writer observes:

> In proof of their indifference to worldly objects, they eat and drink whatever is given them, even *ordure* and *carrion*. They smear their bodies also with excrement, and carry it about with them in a wooden cup, or skull, either to swallow it, if by so doing they can get a few pice, or to throw it upon the persons or into the houses of those who refuse to comply with their demands.—("Religious Sects of the Hindus," in Asiatic Researches, vol. 17, p. 205, Calcutta, India, 1832.)

Another writer confirms the above. The Abbé Dubois says that the Gurus or Indian priests sometimes, as a mark of favor, present to their disciples "the water in which they had washed their feet, which is preserved and sometimes drunk by those who receive it." (Dubois, "People of India," London, 1817, p. 64.) This practice, he tells us, is general among the sectaries of Siva, and is not uncommon with many of the Vishnuites in regard to their vashtuma. "Neither is it the most disgusting of the practices that prevail in that sect of fanatics, as they are under the reproach of eating, as a hallowed morsel, the *very ordure* that proceeds from their *Gurus*, and swallowing the water with which they have rinsed their mouths or washed their faces, with many other practices equally revolting to nature." (*Idem*, p. 71.‡)

That the same disgusting veneration was accorded the person of the Grand Lama, of Thibet, was once generally believed. Maltebrun asserts it in positive terms:

> It is a certain fact that the refuse excreted from his body is collected with sacred solicitude, to be employed as amulets and infallible antidotes to disease.

---

* De Bry, Ind. Orient, in Purchas' Pilgrims, vol. 2, p. 935.

† Comen crudo la carne, y el pescado.—(Gómara, Hist. de las Indias, p. 234.)

‡ Again, on p. 331, Dubois alludes to the "Gynmosophists, or naked Samyasis of India, * * * eating human excrement, without showing the slightest symptom of disgust."

As bearing not unremotely upon this point, the author wishes to say, that in his personal notes and memoranda can be found references to one of the medicine-men of the Sioux, who assured his admirers that everything about him was "medicine," even his excrement, which could be transmuted into copper cartridges.

And, quoting from Pallas, book 1, p. 212, he adds:

Il est hors de doute que le contenu de sa chaise percée est dévotement recueilli; les parties solides sont distribuées comme des amulettes qu'on porte au cou; le liquide est pris intérieurement comme une médécine infallible.—(Maltebrun, Universal Geography, article "Thibet," vol. 2, lib. 45, American edition, Philadelphia, 1832.)

The Abbé Huc denies this assertion:

The Talé Lama is venerated by the Thibetans and the Mongols like a divinity. The influence he exercises over the Buddhist population is truly astonishing; but still it is going too far to say that his excrements are carefully collected and made into amulets, which devotees inclose in pouches and carry around their necks. — (Huc, Travels in Tartary, Thibet, and China, London, 1849, vol. 2, p. 198.)

HUC AND DUBOIS COMPARED.

Huc was a keen and observing traveler; he was well acquainted with the languages and customs of the Mongolians; his tour into Thibet was replete with incident, and his narrative never flags in interest. Still, in Thibet, he was only a traveler; the upper classes of the Buddhist priesthood looked upon him with suspicion. The lower orders of priesthood and people did seem to consider him as a Lama from the far East, but he did not succeed in gaining the confidence of the Thibetans to the extent possessed by Dubois among the Brahminical sects. The history of the latter author is a peculiar one: A French priest, driven from his native land by the excesses of the revolution, he took refuge in India, devoting himself for nearly twenty years to missionary labor among the people, with whom he became so thoroughly identified that when his notes appeared they were published at the expense of the British East India Company, and distributed among its officials as a text-book.

THE MEXICAN GODDESS SUCHIQUECAL EATS ORDURE.

The Mexicans had a goddess, of whom we read the following:

Father Fabreya says, in his commentary on the Codex Borgianus, that the mother of the human race is there represented in a state of humiliation, eating *cuitlatl* (*kopros*, Greek). The vessel in the left hand of Suchiquecal contains "*mierda*," according to the interpreter of these paintings.—(See note to p. 120, Kingsborough's "Mexican Antiquities," vol. 6.)

The Spanish *mierda*, like the Greek *kopros*, means *ordure*.

Deities, created in the ignorance or superstitious fears of devotees, are essentially man-like in their attributes; where they are depicted as cruel and sanguinary toward their enemies, the nation adoring them, no matter how pacific to-day, was once cruel and sanguinary likewise. Anthropophagous gods are worshiped only by the descendants of cannibals, and excrement-eaters only by the progeny of those who were not unacquainted with human *ordure* as an article of food.

THE BACCHIC ORGIES OF THE GREEKS.

The Bacchic orgies of the Greeks, while not strictly assimilated to the ur-orgies, can scarcely be overlooked in this connection.

Montfaucon describes the Omophagi of the Greeks:

Les Omophagies étoient une fête des Grecs qui passoient la fureur Bacchique; ils s'entortilloient, dit Arnobe, de serpens et mangeoient des entrailles de Cabri crues, dont ils avaient la bouche toute ensanglantée; cela est exprimée par le nom Omophage. Nous avons vu quelquefois des hommes tous entortillez de serpens et particulièrement dans Mithras.—(Montfaucon, "L'Antiquité expliquée," tome 2, book 4, p. 22.)

The references to serpent-worship are curious, in view of the fact that such ophic rites still are celebrated among the Mokis, the next-door neighbors of the Zunis, and once existed among the Zunis themselves. The allusion to *Mithras* would seem to imply that these orgies must have been known to the Persians as well as the Greeks.

Bryant, speaking of the Greek orgies, uses this language:

Both in the orgies of Bacchus and in the rites of Ceres, as well as of other deities, one part of the mysteries consisted in a ceremony (*omophagia*), at which time they ate the flesh quite crude with the blood. In Crete, at the Dionisiaca, they used to tear the flesh with their teeth from the animal when alive.—(Bryant, "Mythology," London, 1775, vol. 2, p. 12.)

And again, on p. 13:

The Maenules and Bacchæ used to devour the raw limbs of animals which they had cut or torn asunder. * * In the island of Chios it was a religious custom to tear a man limb from limb, by way of sacrifice to Dionysius. From all which we may learn one sad truth, that there is scarce anything so impious and unnatural as not, at times, to have prevailed.—(*Idem.*)

Faber tells us that—

The Cretans had an annual festival * * * in their frenzy they tore a living bull with their teeth, and brandished serpents in their hands.—(Faber, "Pagan Idolatry," London, 1816, vol. 2, p. 265.)

BACCHIC ORGIES IN NORTH AMERICA.

These orgies were duplicated among many of the tribes of North America. Paul Kane describes the inauguration of Clea-clach, a Clallum chief (Northwest coast of British America); "he seized a small dog and began devouring it alive." He also bit pieces from the shoulders of the male by-standers. (See "Artist's Wanderings in North America," London, 1859, p. 212; also, the same thing quoted by Herbert Spencer, in "Descriptive Sociology.")

Bancroft describes like orgies among the Chimsyans, of British North America. (See in "Native Races of the Pacific Slope," vol. 1, p. 171.) While the Nootkas medicine-men are said to have an orgie in which "live dogs and dead human bodies are seized and torn by their teeth; but, at least in later times, they seem not to attack the living, and their performances are somewhat less horrible and bloody than the wild orgies of the northern tribes." (*Idem*, vol. 1, p. 202.)

The Haidahs, of the same coast, indulge in an orgie in which the performer "snatches up the first dog he can find, kills him, and tearing pieces of his flesh, eats them." (Dall, quoting Dawson, in "Masks and Labrets," Annual Report of the Bureau of Ethnology, Washington, D. C., 1886.)

In describing the six secret soldier societies or bands of the Mandans, Maximilian, of Wied, calls attention to the three leaders of one band, who were called dogs, who are "obliged, if any one throws a piece of meat into the ashes or on the ground, saying, 'There, dog, eat,' to fall upon it and devour it raw, like dogs or beasts of prey." (Maximilian, Prince of Wied, "Travels," &c., London, 1843, pp. 356, 446.)

A further multiplication of references is unnecessary. The above would appear to be enough to establish the existence of almost identical orgies in Europe, America, and Asia—orgies in which were perpetuated the ritualistic use of foods no longer employed by the populace, and possibly commemorating a former condition of cannibalism.

THE SACRIFICE OF THE DOG A SUBSTITUTION FOR HUMAN SACRIFICE.

It would add much to the bulk of this chapter to show that the dog has almost invariably been employed as a substitute for man in sacrifice. Other animals have performed the same vicarious office, but none to the same extent, especially among the more savage races. To the American Indians and other peoples of a corresponding stage of development the substitution presents no logical incongruity. Their religious conceptions are so strongly tinged with *zoolatry* that the assignment of animals to the *rôle* of deities or of victims is the most natural thing in the world; but their belief is not limited to the idea that the animal is sacred—it comprehends, additionally, a settled appreciation of the fact that *lycanthropy* is possible, and that the medicine-men possess the power of transforming men into animals or animals into men. Such a belief was expressed to the writer in the most forcible way, in the village of Zuni, in 1881. The Indians were engaged in some one of their countless dances and ceremonies (and possibly not very far from the time of the urine dance), when the dancers seized a small dog and tore it limb from limb, venting upon it every torture that savage spite and malignity could devise. The explanation given was, that the hapless cur was a "Navajo," a tribe with which the Zunis have been spasmodically hostile for generations, and from whose ranks the fortunes of war must have enabled them to drag an occasional captive to be put to the torture and sacrificed.

URINE IN HUMAN FOOD—CHINOOK OLIVES.

The addition of urine to human food is mentioned by various writers. Speaking of the Chinooks, Paul Kane describes a delicacy manufactured by some of the Indians among whom he traveled, and called by him "Chinook olives." They were nothing more or less than acorns soaked for five months in human urine. (Kane, "Artist's Wanderings in North America," London, 1859, p. 187.) Spencer copies Kane's story in his Descriptive Sociology, article "Chinooks.".

URINE USED IN BREAD-MAKING.

A comparatively late writer says of the Mokis of Arizona:

> They are not as clean in their housekeeping as the Navajoes, and it is hinted that they sometimes mix their meal with chamber-lye for these festive occasions, but I did not know that until I talked with Mormons who had visited them.—(J. H. Beadle, "Western Wilds," Cincinnati, Ohio, 1878, p. 279.)

Beadle lived and ate with the Mokis for a number of days. This story, coming from the Mormons, may refer to some imperfectly understood ceremonial.

URINE USED IN THE MANUFACTURE OF SALT.

Gómara explains that, mixed with palm-scrapings, human urine served as salt to the Indians of Bogota.*

SIBERIAN HOSPITALITY.

A curious manifestation of hospitality has been noticed among the Tchuktchi of Siberia:

> Las Tschuktschi offrent leurs femmes aux voyageurs; mais ceux-ci, pour s'en rendre dignes, doivent se soumettre à une epreuve dégoutante. La fille ou la femme qui doit passer la nuit avec son nouvel hôte lui présente une tasse pleine de son urine; il faut qu'il s'en rince la bouche. S'il a ce courage, il est regardé comme un ami sincère; sinon, il est traité comme un ennemi de la famille.—(Dulaure. "Des Divinités Génératrices," Paris, 1825, p. 400.)

* Hacen sal de raspaduras de palma y orinas de hombre.—(Gómara, Historia de las Indias, p. 202.)

The presentation of women to distinguished strangers is a mark of savage hospitality noted all over the world, but never in any other place with the above peculiar accompaniment; yet, Mungo Park assures his readers that, during his travels in the interior of Africa, a wedding occurred among the Moors while he was asleep. He was awakened from his doze by an old woman bearing a wooden bowl, whose contents she discharged full in his face, saying it was a present from the bride.

Finding this to be the same sort of holy water with which a Hottentot priest is said to sprinkle a newly-married couple, he supposed it to be a mischievous frolic, but was informed that it was a nuptial benediction from the bride's own person, and which, on such occasions, is always received by the young unmarried Moors as a mark of distinguished favor.—(Quoted in Brand, Popular Antiquities, London, 1849, vol. 2, p. 152, article "Bride-Ales." See, also, Mungo Park's "Travels in Africa," New York, 1813, p. 109.)

In the last two citations religious or at least superstitious motives obtrude themselves; those to follow show these in a much more marked degree.

POISONOUS MUSHROOMS USED IN UR–ORGIES.

The Indians in and around Cape Flattery, on the Pacific coast of British North America, retain the urine dance in an unusually repulsive form. As was learned from Mr. Kennard, U. S. Coast Survey, whom the writer had the pleasure of meeting in Washington, D. C., in 1886, the medicine men distil, from potatoes and other ingredients, a vile liquor, which has an irritating and exciting effect upon the kidneys and bladder. Each one who has partaken of this dish immediately urinates and passes the result to his next neighbor, who drinks. The effect is as above, and likewise a temporary insanity or delirium, during which all sorts of mad capers are carried on. The last man who quaffs the poison, distilled through the persons of five or six comrades, is so completely overcome that he falls in a dead stupor.

Precisely the same use of a poisonous fungus has been described among the natives of the Pacific coast of Siberia, according to the learned Dr. J. W. Kingsley (of Brome Hall, Scole, England). Such a rite is outlined by Schultze. "The Shamans of Siberia drink a decoction of toad-stools or the urine of those who have become narcotized by that plant." (Schultze, "Fetichism," New York, 1885, p. 52.*)

* Corroborative testimony was also received by the author from Mr. George Kennan, of Washington, D. C., who lived for three years among the Tchuktchi, Baruts, and Yakuts of Siberia.

A SIMILAR USE OF FUNGI QUITE PROBABLY EXISTED AMONG THE MEXICANS.

That some such use of poisonous fungi was made by other nations would be difficult to prove in the absence of direct testimony; but many incidental references are encountered which the reflective mind must consider with care before rejecting as absolutely irrelevant in this connection. The Mexicans, as we learn from Sahagun, were not ignorant of the mushroom, which is described as the basis of one of their festivals. He says that they ate the nanacatl, a poisonous fungus which intoxicated as much as wine; after eating it, they assembled in a plain, where they danced and sang by night and by day to their fullest desire. This was on the first day, because on the following day they all wept bitterly, and they said that they were cleaning themselves and washing their eyes and faces with their tears.*

It is true that Sahagun does not describe any specially revolting feature in this orgie, but it is equally patent that he is describing from hearsay, and, probably, was not allowed to know too much. In a second reference to this fungus, which he now calls teo-nanacatl, he alludes to the toxic properties, which coincide closely with those of the mushrooms noted in Siberia and on the northwest coast of America:

> There are some mushrooms in this country which are called teo-nanacatl. They grow under the grass in the fields and plains; * * * they are hurtful to the throat and intoxicate; * * * those who eat them see visions and feel flutterings in the heart; those who eat many of them are excited to lust, and even so if they eat but few.†

The proof is not at all conclusive that this intoxication was produced as among the Siberian and Cape Flattery tribes; but it is very odd that the Aztecs should eat mushrooms for the same purpose; that they should hold their dance out in a plain and by night (that is, in a place as remote as possible from Father Sahagun's inspection). On the second day, to trust Sahagun's explanation, they would appear to have bewailed their behavior on the first; although it should be remarked here that ceremonial weeping has not been unknown to the American aborigines, and

*Nanacatl, que son los hongos malos que emborrachan tan bien como el vino; y se juntaban en un llano despues de haberlo comido, donde bailaban y cantaban de noche y de dia á su placer; y esto el primer dia porque al dia siguiente lloraban todos mucho y decian que se limpiaban y lavaban los ojos y caras con sus lagrimas.—(Sahagun, in Kingsborough's "Mexican Antiquities," vol. 7, p. 308.)

†Hay unos honguillos en esta tierra que se llaman teo-nanacatl; crianse debajo del heno en los campos ó páramos * * * dañan la garganta y emborrachan * * * los que los comen ven visiones y sienten buscas eu el corazon; á los que comen muchos de ellos provocan á luxuria, y aunque sean pocos.—(Sahagun, in Kingsborough's "Mexican Antiquities," vol. 7, p. 369.)

may, in this case, have been induced by causes not revealed to the stranger. Lastly, it is important to note that this poisonous fungus was a violent excitant, a nervous irritant, and an aphrodisiac.

Another early Spanish observer, also cited by Kingsborough, describes them in these terms:

> They had another kind of drunkenness, * * * which was with small fungi or mushrooms, * * * which are eaten raw, and, on account of being bitter, they drink after them or eat with them a little honey of bees, and shortly after that they see a thousand visions, especially snakes.

They went raving mad, running about the streets in a wild state ("bestial embriaguez"). They called these fungi "teo-na-m-catl," a word meaning "bread of the gods."

This author does not allude to any effect upon the kidneys.*

The list of quotations is not yet complete. Tezozomoc, also an author of repute, relates that at the coronation of Montezuma the Mexicans gave wild mushrooms to the strangers to eat; that the strangers became drunk, and thereupon began to dance.† All of which is a terse description of a drunken orgie induced by poisonous mushrooms, but not represented with the disgusting sequences which would have served to establish a connection with urine dances.

Diego Duran also gives the particulars of the coronation of this Montezuma (the second of the name and the one on the throne at the date of the arrival of Cortés). He says that, after the usual human sacrifices had been offered up in the temples, all went to eat raw mushrooms, which caused them to lose their senses and affected them more than if they had drunk much wine. So utterly beside themselves were they that many of them killed themselves with their own hands, and by the potency of those mushrooms they saw visions and had revelations of the future, the devil speaking to them in their drunkenness.‡ Duran, of course, is not

* Tenian otra manera de embriaguez * * * era con unos hongos ó setas pequeñas * * * que comidos crudos y por ser amargos, beben tras ellos ó comen con ellos un poco de miel de abejas, y de alli á poco rato, veian mil visiones y en especial culebras.—(By the author of "Ritos Antiguos, Sacrificios é idolatrias de los Indios en Nueva España," Kingsborough, vol. ix, p. 17.)

This author seems to have been the Franciscan Fray Toribio de Benvento, commonly called by his Aztec nickname of "Motolinia, the Beggar." He is designated by Kingsborough "the Unknown Franciscan," because, through motives of humility, he declined to subscribe his name to his valuable writings.

† Á los estranjeros, les diéron á comer hongos montesinos que se embriagaban con ellos y con esto entráron á la danza.—(Tezozomoc, "Cronica Mexicana," in Kingsborough, "Mexican Antiquities," vol. 9, p. 153.)

‡ Ivan todos á comer hongos crudos, con la cual comida salian todos de juicio y quedaban peores que si hubieran bebido mucho vino tan embriagados y fuera de sentido que muchos de ellos se mataban con propria mano; y con la fuerza de aquellos hongos vian visiones y tenian rebelaciones de lo porvenir hablandoles el Demonio en aquella embriaguez.—(Diego Duran, lib. 2, cap. 54, p. 564.)

describing what he *saw*. Doubtless, in that case, his narrative would have been more animated and, possibly, more to our purpose.

MUSHROOMS AND TOADSTOOLS WORSHIPED BY AMERICAN INDIANS.

Dorman is authority for the statement that mushrooms were worshiped by the Indians of the Antilles, and toad-stools by those in Virginia,* but for what toxic or therapeutic qualities, real or supposed, he does not say.

A FORMER USE OF FUNGUS INDICATED IN THE MYTHS OF CEYLON, AND IN THE LAWS OF THE BRAHMINS.

On the west shore of the Pacific Ocean, aside from the orgies of the Siberian Shamans, no instance is on record of the use of the mushroom or other fungus in religious rites in the present day.

A former use of it is indicated in the Cingalese myths, which teach that—

Chance produced a species of mushroom called mattika † or jessathon, on which they lived for sixty-five thousand years; but, being determined to make an equal division of this, also, they lost it. Luckily for them, another creeping plant [mistletoe?] called badrilata grew up, on which they (the Brahmins) fed for thirty-five thousand years, but which they lost for the same reason as the former ones.—(Asiatic Researches, Calcutta, 1807, vol. 7, p. 441.)

Among the Brahmins of the main-land no such myth is related; but an English writer says:

The ancient Hindus held the fungus in such detestation that Yama, a legislator, supposed now to be the judge of departed spirits, declares: "Those who eat mushrooms, whether springing from the ground or growing on a tree, fully equal in guilt to the slayers of Brahmins and the most despicable of all deadly sinners."—(Asiatic Researches, Calcutta, 1795, vol. 4, p. 311.)

Dubois refers to the same subject. The Brahmins, he says—

Have also retrenched from their vegetable food, which is the great fund of their subsistence, all roots which form a head or bulb in the ground, such as onions,‡ and those

* Rushton M. Dorman, "Primitive Superstitions," New York, 1881, p. 295.

† The word "mattika" cannot be found in Forbes' English-Hindustani Dictionary (London. 1848.) It may, perhaps, belong to an extinct dialect. The word "matt," meaning "drunk," would serve a good purpose for this article could a relationship be shown to exist between it and mattika. This the author is of course unable to do, being totally ignorant of Hindustani. Neither does "badrilata" occur in Forbes, who interprets "mistletoe" as "banda." The contributor to the Asiatic Researches, who used the word, though it meant "agaric."

‡ Higgins believes that the ancient Egyptians had discovered similarity between the coats of an onion and the planetary spheres, and says that it was called (by the Greeks), from being sacred to the father of ages, oionoon—onion. * * * The onion was adored (as the black stone in Westminster Abbey is by us) by the Egyptians for this property, as a type of the eternal renewal of ages. * * * The onion is adored in India, and forbidden to be eaten.—(Quoting Forster's Sketches of Hindoos, p. 35, Higgins' Anacalypsis, vol. 2, p. 427.)

also which assume the same shape above ground, like mushrooms and some others. * * * Are we to suppose that they had discovered something unwholesome in the one species and prescribed the other on account of its fetid smell? This I cannot decide; all the information I have ever obtained from those among them whom I have consulted on the reasons of their abstinence from them being that it is customary to avoid such articles.—(Abbé Dubois, "People of India," London, 1817, p. 117.)

This inhibition, under such dire penalties, can have but one meaning. In primitive times, the people of India must have been so addicted to the debauchery induced by potions into the composition of which entered poisonous fungi and mistletoe (the mushroom "growing on a tree") and the effects of such debauchery must have been found so debasing and pernicious that the priest-rulers were compelled to employ the same maledictions which Moses proved of efficacy in withdrawing the children of Israel from the worship of idols.*

AN INQUIRY INTO THE DRUIDICAL USE OF THE MISTLETOE.

But the question at once presents itself, for what reason did the Celtic Druids employ the much-venerated mistletoe? This question becomes of deep significance in the light of the learning shed by Godfrey Higgins and General Vallencey upon the derivation of the Druids from a Buddhistic or Brahminical origin.†

That the mistletoe was regarded as a medicine, and a very potent one, is easy enough to show. All the encyclopædias admit that much, but the accounts that have been preserved of the ideas associated with this worship are not complete or satisfactory.

The mistletoe, which they (the Druids) called "all-heal," used to cure disease.—(McClintock and Strong's Encyclopædia, quoting Stukeley.)

Within recent times the mistletoe has been regarded as a valuable remedy in epilepsy [Query: On the principle of *similia similibus?*] and other diseases, but at present is not employed. * * * The leaves have been fed to sheep in time of scarcity of other forage. [Which shows, at least, that it is edible.]—(Appleton's American Encyclopædia.)

Seems to possess no decided medicinal properties.—(International Encyclopædia.)

Pliny mentions three varieties; of these—

The hyphar is useful for fattening cattle, if they are hardy enough to withstand the purgative effects it produces at first. * * * The viscum is medicinally of value as an emollient, and in cases of tumors, ulcers, and the like.

* But on the 6th day of the moon's age "women walk in the forests with a fan in one hand and eat *certain vegetables*, in hope of beautiful children. See the account given by Pliny of the Druidical mistletoe or viscum, which was to be gathered when the moon was six days old, as a preservative from sterility."—(Sir William Jones, in Asiatic Researches, Calcutta, 1790, vol. 3, art. 12, p. 284; quoted by Edward Moor, "Hindu Pantheon," London, 1810, p. 134.)

† It is now, perhaps, impossible to account for the veneration in which it was held and the wonderful qualities which it was supposed to possess.—("The Druids," Reverend Richard Smiddy, Dublin, 1871, p. 90.)

Pliny is also quoted as saying that it was considered of benefit to women in childbirth—"in conceptum feminarum adjuvare si omnino secum habeant."* Pliny is also authority for the reverence in which the mistletoe growing on the robur (Spanish "roble," or evergreen oak) was held by the Druids. The robur, he says, is their sacred tree, and whatever is found growing upon it they regard as sent from heaven, and as the mark of a tree chosen by God. (Encyclopædia Britannica.)

Brand (Popular Antiquities, London, 1849, vol. 1, art. "Mistletoe") cites the opinion of various old authors that mistletoe was regarded "as a medicine very likely to subdue not only the epilepsy, but all other convulsive disorders. * * * The high veneration in which the Druids were held by the people of all ranks proceeded in a great measure from the wonderful cures they wrought by means of the mistletoe of the oak. * * * The mistletoe of the oak, which is very rare, is vulgarly said to be a cure for wind-ruptures in children; the kind which is found upon the apple is said to be good for fits."

Much testimony may be adduced to show that the mistletoe was valued as an aphrodisiac, as conducive to fertility, as sacred to love, and, in general terms, an excitant of the genito-urinary organs, which is the very purpose for which the Siberian and North American medicine-men employed the fungus, and perhaps the very reason for which both fungus and mistletoe were excluded from the Brahminical dietary.

Brand shows that mistletoe "was not unkown in the religious ceremonies of the ancients, particularly the Greeks," and that the use of it, savoring strongly of Druidism, prevailed at the Christmas service of York Cathedral down to our own day. (See in Brand, Popular Antiquities, London, 1849, vol. 1, p. 524.)

The merry pastime of kissing pretty girls under the Christmas mistletoe seems to have a phallic derivation. "This very old custom has descended from feudal times, but its real origin and significance are lost." (Appleton's American Encyclopædia.) Brand shows that the young men observed the custom of "plucking off a berry at each kiss." (Vol. 1, p. 524.) Perhaps, in former times, they were required to swallow the berry.

A writer in Notes and Queries (January 3, 1852, vol. 5, p. 13) quotes Nares, to the effect that "the maid who was not kissed under it at

---

* **Montfaucon says of the Druids: "Ils croient que les animaux steriles deviennent féconds en buvant de l'eau de Gui."—(L'antiquité Expliquée, Paris, 1722, tome 2, part 2, p. 436—quoting and translating Pliny.)**

Christmas would not be married in that year." But another writer (February 28, 1852, same volume) points out that "we should refer the custom to the Scandinavian mythology, wherein the mistletoe is dedicated to Friga, the Venus of the Scandinavians."*

Another writer (Notes and Queries, 2d series, vol. 4, p. 506) says:

As it was supposed to possess the mystic power of giving fertility and a power to preserve from poison, the pleasant ceremony of kissing under the mistletoe may have some reference to this belief.

In vol. 3, p. 343, it is stated:

A Worcestershire farmer was accustomed to take down his bough of mistletoe and give it to the cow that calved first after New Year's Day. This was supposed to insure good luck to the whole dairy. Cows, it may be remarked, as well as sheep, will devour mistletoe with avidity.

And still another, in 2d series, vol. 6, p. 523, recognizes that "the mistletoe was sacred to the heathen goddess of Beauty," and "it is certain that the mistletoe, though it formerly had a place among the evergreens employed in the Christian decorations, was subsequently excluded." This exclusion he accounts for thus:

It is also certain that, in the earlier ages of the church, many festivities not at all tending to edification (the practice of mutual kissing among the rest) had gradually crept in and established themselves; so that, at a certain part of the service, "statim clerus, ipseque populus per basia blande sese invicim oscularetur."

This author cites Hone, Hook, Moroni, Bescherelle, Ducange, and others. Finally, in the 3d series, vol. 7, p. 76, an inquirer asks "how came it, in Shakespeare's time, to be considered 'baleful,' and, in our days, the most mirth-provoking of plants;" and still another correspondent, in same series, vol. 7, p. 237, claims that "mistletoe will produce abortion in the female of the deer or dog."

FORMER EMPLOYMENT OF AN INFUSION OR DECOCTION OF MISTLETOE.

That an infusion or decoction of the plant was once in use may be gathered from the fact narrated by John Eliot Howard:

Water, in which the sacred mistletoe had been immersed, was given to or sprinkled upon the people.—("The Druids and their Religion," John Eliot Howard, in Transactions of Victoria Institute, vol. 14, p. 118, quoting "Le gui de chêne et les Druides," E. Magdaleine, Paris, 1877.†)

---

* It was the only plant in the world which could harm Baldur, the son of Odin and Friga. When a branch of it struck him he fell dead.—(See in Bullfinch's Mythology, revised by Reverend E. E. Hale, Boston, 1883, p. 428.)

"When found growing on the oak," the mistletoe "represented man."—(Opinion of the French writer Reynaud, in his article "Druidism," quoted in the Encyclopædia Britannica.)

†See notes on the Hindu Lingam of this monograph.

THE MISTLETOE ALLEGED TO HAVE BEEN HELD SACRED BY THE MOUND-BUILDERS.

An American writer says, that among the Mound-builders the mistletoe was "the holiest and most rare of evergreens," and that when human sacrifices were offered to sun and moon the victim was covered with mistletoe, which was burnt as an incense. (Pidgeon, "Dee-coo-dah," New York, 1853, p. 91, &c.) Pidgeon claimed to receive his knowledge from Indians versed in the traditions and lore of their tribes.*

Mrs. Eastman presents a drawing of what may be taken as the altar of Haokah, the anti-natural God of the Sioux, in which is a representation of a "large fungus that grows on trees" (query, mistletoe?), which, if eaten by an animal, will cause its death.†

THE MISTLETOE FESTIVAL OF THE MEXICANS.

That the Mexicans had a reverence for the mistletoe would seem to be assured. They had a mistletoe festival. In October they celebrated the festival of the Neypachtly, or bad eye, which was a plant growing on trees and hanging from them, gray with the dampness of rain; especially did it grow on the different kinds of oak.‡ The informant says he can give no explanation of this festival.

VESTIGES OF DRUIDICAL RITES IN FRANCE AT PRESENT DAY.

It may be interesting to detect vestiges of Druidical rites tenaciously adhering to the altered life of modern civilization.

> In the department of Seine et Oise, twelve leagues from Paris (says a recent writer), when a child had a rupture (hernia) he was brought under a certain oak, and some women, who no doubt earned a living in that trade, danced around the oak, muttering spell-words till the child was cured, that is, dead.—(Notes and Queries, 5th series, vol. 7, p. 163.)

It has already been shown that the Druids ascribed this very medical quality to the mistletoe of the oak.

Other curious instances of survival present themselves in the linguistics of the subject. The French word "gui," meaning mistletoe, is not of

---

*See also Ellen Russell Emerson, "Indian Myths," Boston, 1884, p. 331, wherein Pidgeon is quoted.

†"Legends of the Sioux," Eastman, New York, 1849, p. 210. Readers interested in the subject of Indian altars will find descriptions, with colored plates, in the coming work of Surgeon Washington Matthews, U. S. Army, and in the "Snake dance of the Moquis of Arizona," by the author.

‡Neypachtly, quiere decir "mal ojo;" es una yerva que nace en los arboles y cuelga de ellos, parda con la humedad de las aguas, especialmente se cria en los encinales y robles.—(Diego Duran, vol. 3, cap. 16, p. 391½. Manuscript copy in Congressional Library, Washington, D. C.)

Latin but of Druidical derivation, and so the Spanish "aguinaldo," meaning Christmas or New Year's present, conserves the cry, slightly altered, of the Druid priest to the "gui" at the opening of the new year.

COW DUNG AND COW URINE IN RELIGION.

The sacrificial value of cow dung and cow urine throughout India and Thibet is much greater than the reader might be led to infer from the brief citation already noted from Max Müller.

Hindu merchants in Bokhara now lament loudly at the sight of a piece of cow's flesh, and at same time mix with their food that it may do them good the urine of a sacred cow kept in that place.—(Erman, "Siberia," London, 1848, vol. 1, p. 384.)

Picart narrates that the Brahmans fed grain to a sacred cow and afterward searched in the ordure for the sacred grains, which they picked out whole, drying them and administering to the sick not merely as a medicine, but as a sacred thing.*

Not only among the people of the lowlands, but among those of the foot-hills of the Himalayas as well, do these rites find place; "the very dung of the cow is eaten as an atonement for sin, and its urine is used in worship." (Notes on the Hill Tribes of the Neilgherries, Short, Trans. Ethnol. Society, London, 1868, p. 268.)

The greatest, or, at any rate, the most convenient of all purifiers is the urine of a cow; * * * images are sprinkled with it. No man of any pretentions to piety or cleanliness would pass a cow in the act of staling without receiving the holy stream in his hand and sipping a few drops. * * * If the animal be retentive, a pious expectant will impatiently apply his finger, and by judicious tickling excite the grateful flow.—(Moor's "Hindu Pantheon," London, 1810, p. 143.)

Dubois, in his chapter "Restoration to the Caste," says that a Hindu penitent "must drink the *panchakaryam*—a word which literally signifies the five things, namely, milk, butter, curd, dung, and urine, all mixed together," and he adds:

The urine of the cow is held to be the most efficacious of any for purifying all imaginable uncleanness. I have often seen the superstitious Hindu accompanying these animals

*Après avoir donné du riz en pot, à manger aux vaches ils vont fouiller dans la bouze et en retirent les grains qu'ils trouvent entiers. Ils font sécher ces grains et les donnent à leurs malades, non seulement comme un remède mais encore comme une chose sainte.—(Picart, "Coûtumes et Cérémonies réligieuses," &c., Amsterdam, 1729, vol. 7, p. 18.)

This is neither better nor worse than the custom of the Indians of Texas, Florida, and California, herein before described.

Chez les Indiens, la bouze de la vache est très sainte.—(Picart, *Idem*, vol. 6, part 2, p. 191-193.)

Picart also discloses that the Banians swear by a cow.—(*Idem*, vol. 7, p. 16.)

The author of this article learned while campaigning with General Crook against the hostile Sioux and Cheyennes in 1876 and 1877 that the Sioux and Assinniboines had a form of oath sworn to while the affiant held in each hand a piece of buffalo chip.

A small quantity of the urine (of the cow) is daily sipped by some (of the Hindus).—(Asiatic Researches, Calcutta, 1805, vol. 8, p. 81.)

when in the pasture and watching the moment for receiving the urine as it fell in vessels which he had brought for the purpose, to carry it home in a fresh state; or, catching it in the hollow of his hand, to bedew his face and all his body. When so used, it removes all external impurity, and when taken internally, which is very common, it cleanses all within.—(Abbé Dubois, "People of India," London, 1817, p. 29.)

Very frequently the excrement is first reduced to ashes. The monks of Chivem, called Pandarones, smear their faces, breasts, and arms with the ashes of cow dung; they run through the streets demanding alms, very much as the Zuni actors demanded a feast, and chant the praises of Chivem, while they carry a bundle of peacock feathers in the hand and wear the *lingam* at the neck.*

COW DUNG ALSO USED BY THE ISRAELITES.

In another place Dulaure calls attention to the similar use among the Hebrews of the ashes of the dung of the red heifer as an expiatory sacrifice.†

HUMAN ORDURE USED IN FOOD BY THE ISRAELITES.

Among the Banians of India proselytes are obliged by the Brahmans to eat cow dung for six months. They begin with one pound daily, and diminish from day to day. A subtle commentator, says Picart, might institute a comparison between the nourishment of these fanatics and the dung of cows which the Lord ordered the prophet Ezekiel to mingle with his food.‡

This was the opinion held by Voltaire on this subject. Speaking of the prophet Ezekiel, he said, "He is to eat bread of barley, wheat, beans, lentils, and millet, and to cover it with human excrement." It is thus, he says, that the "children of Israel shall eat their bread defiled among the nations among which they shall be banished." But, "after having

---

* Les moines de Chivem sont nommés Pandarons. Ils se barbouillent le visage, la poitrine, et les bras avec des cendres de bouse de vache: ils parcourent les rues, demandent l'aumône et chantent les louanges de Chivem, en portant un paquet de plumes de paon à la main et le lingam pendu au cou.—(Dulaure, "Des Divinités génératrices," Paris, 1825, p. 105.)

† Les Hebreux sacrifiaient et faisaient brûler la vache rousse, dont les cendres mêlées avec de l'eau servaient aux expiations. Chez les Indiens, les cendres de la bouse de vache sont également employées aux expiations.—(Dulaure, *idem*, chap. 1, pp. 23, 24.)

They shall burn in the fire their dung.—(Levit., xvi: 27.)

Her blood with her dung shall he burn.—(Numbers, xix: 5.)

‡ Disons un mot de la manière dont les Proselytes des Banians sont obligés de vivre les premiers mois de leur conversion. Les Brahmines leur ordonnent de mêler de la fiente de la vache dans tout ce qu'ils mangent pendant ce tems de régénération. * * * Que ne diroit pas ici un commentateur subtil qui voudroit comparer la nourriture de ces proselytes avec les ordres que Dieu donna autrefois à Ezechiel de mêler de la fiente de vache dans ses alimens. Ezekiel, iv.—(Picart. "Côutumes et cérémonies réligieuses," &c., Amsterdam, 1729, vol. 7, p. 15.) "And thou shalt eat it as barley cakes, and thou shalt eat it with dung that cometh out of man, in their sight."—(Ezekiel, iv: 12.)

eaten this bread of affliction, God permits him to cover it with the excrement of cattle simply." *

The view entertained by some biblical commentators is that the excrement was used for baking the bread; but if this be true, why should human fæces be used for such a purpose. (Consult Lange's Commentaries, article "Ezekiel," and McClintock and Strong's Cyclopædia, article "Dung.")

There is also a purification of the soul of the dying by the same peculiar methods. In Coromandel, the dying man is so placed that his face will come under the tail of a cow; the tail is lifted and the cow excited to void her urine. If the urine fall upon the face of the sick man, the people cry out with joy, considering him to be one of the blessed, but if the sacred animal be in no humor to gratify their wishes, they are greatly afflicted.†

Monier Williams repeats almost what Müller says about the Parsis. A young Parsi undergoes a sort of confirmation, during which "he is made to drink a small quantity of the urine of a bull." (Monier Williams, "Modern India," London, 1878, p. 178.) And in describing the cremation of a Hindoo corpse at Bombay, the same author relates that the ashes of the pyre were sprinkled with water, a cake of cow dung placed in the center, and around it a small stream of cow urine; upon this were placed plantain leaves, rice-cakes, and flowers. ("Modern India," p. 65.)

THE ASSYRIAN VENUS HAD OFFERINGS OF DUNG PLACED UPON HER ALTARS.

Another authority states that "the zealous adorers of Siva rub the forehead, breast, and shoulders with ashes of cow dung;" and further he adds:

> It is very remarkable that the Assyrian Venus, according to Lucian, had also offerings of dung placed upon her altars.—(Maurice, "Indian Antiquities," London, 1800, vol. 1, pp. 172, 173.)

Speaking of the sacrifice called Poojah, Maurice says:

> The Brahman prepares a place which is purified with dried cow dung, with which the pavement is spread, and the room is sprinkled with the urine of the same animal.—(*Idem*, vol. 1, p. 77.)

---

* "Il doit manger du pain du froment, d'orge, de fêves, de lentilles, de millets et le couvrir d'excrémens humains." etc.—(Voltaire, Essais sur les Moeurs, vol. 1, p. 195, Paris, 1785.)

† Au Coromandel, ils mettent le visage du mourant sur le derriére d'une vache, lévent la queue de l'animal et l'exciteut à lacher son uriue sur le visage * * * si l'urine coule sur la face du malade, l'assemblée s'écrie de joye et le compte parmi les bienheureux, mais * * * si la vache n'est pas d'humeur d'uriner, on s'en afflige.—(Picart, "Coûtumes et cérémonies réligieuses," &c., Amsterdam, 1729, vol. 7, p. 28.)

In one of the Hindu fasts the devotee adopts these disgusting excreta as his food. On the fourth day "his disgusting beverage is the urine of the cow; the fifth, the excrement of that holy animal is his allotted food." (Maurice, "Indian Antiquities," London, 1800, vol. 5, p. 222.)

Maurice cites five meritorious kinds of suicide, in the second of which the Hindu devotee is described as "covering himself with cow dung, setting it on fire, and consuming himself therein." (Maurice, "Indian Antiquities," London, 1800, vol. 2, p. 49.*)

Doors of houses are smeared with cow dung and nimba leaves, as a preservative from poisonous reptiles. (Moor's "Hindu Pantheon," London, 1810, p. 23.)

THE SACRED COW'S EXCRETA A SUBSTITUTE FOR HUMAN SACRIFICE.

The foregoing testimony, which could readily be swelled in volume, proves the sacred character of these excreta, which may be looked upon as substitutes for a more perfect sacrifice. In the early life of the Hindus it is more than likely that the cow or the heifer was slaughtered by the knife or burnt; as population increased in density, domestic cattle became too costly to be offered as a frequent oblation, and on the principle that the part represents the whole, hair, milk, butter, urine, and ordure superseded the slain carcass, while the incinerated excrement was made to do duty as a burnt sacrifice.†

It was hardly probable that such practices, or an explanation of the causes which led to their adoption and perpetuation, should have escaped the keen criticism of E. B. Tylor. He says:

> For the means of some of his multifarious lustrations, the Hindu has recourse to the sacred cow. * * * The Parsi religion prescribes a system of lustration which well shows its common origin with that of Hinduism by its similar use of cow's urine and water. * * * Applications of "*nirang*," washed off with water, form part of the daily religious rites, as well as of such special ceremonies as the naming of the new-born child, the putting on of the sacred cord, the purification of the mother after childbirth, and the purification of him who has touched a corpse.—(E. B. Tylor, "Primitive Culture," London, 1871, vol. 2, pp. 396, 397.)

---

* The Hebrew prophets bedaubed themselves with ordure and sat on dung-heaps, while the recalcitrant people of Israel were warned: "Behold, I will spread dung upon your faces, even *the dung of your solemn feasts*, and one shall take you away with it."—(Malachi, 2: 3.)

†Such an economic tendency in the sacrificial practices of the Parsis is shown by Tylor. The Vedic sacrifice, Agnishtoma, required that animals should be slain and their flesh partly committed to the gods by fire, partly eaten by sacrificers and priests. The Parsi ceremony, Izeshne, formal successor of this bloody rite, requires no animal to be killed, but it suffices to place the hair of an ox in a vessel and show it to the fire.—(Primitive Culture, E. B. Tylor, New York, 1874, vol. 2, p. 400.)

This citation is valuable because it supports with such authority the conclusion which must have entered the minds of all who have scanned these pages, that the Parsi and Brahminical ceremonials are offshoots from a common stock. But of even greater value is the testimony, also collected by Tylor, in regard to substitutive sacrifices, in which the fact is made to appear that the sacred cow of India takes the place originally occupied by a human victim.* His explanation is of such interest that space may well be claimed for it in this chapter:

It will help us to realize how the sacrifice of an animal may atone for a human life, if we notice in South Africa how a Zulu will redeem a lost child from the finder by a bullock, or a Kimbunda will expiate the blood of a slave by the offering of an ox, whose blood will wash away the other. For instances of the animal substituted for man in sacrifice, the following may serve: Among the Khonds of Orissa, where Colonel MacPherson was engaged in putting down the sacrifice of human victims by the sect of the Earth-goddess, they at once began to discuss the plan of sacrificing cattle by way of substitutes. Now, there is some reason to think that this same course of ceremonial change may account for the following sacrificial practice in the other Khond sect. It appears that those who worship the Light-god hold a festival in his honor, when they slaughter a buffalo in commemoration of the time when, as they say, the Earth-goddess was prevailing on men to offer human sacrifices to her, but the Light-god sent a tribe-deity who crushed the bloody-minded Earth-goddess under a mountain and dragged a buffalo out of the jungle, saying: "Liberate the man and sacrifice the buffalo." It looks as though this legend, divested of its mythic garb, may really record a historical substitution of animal for human sacrifice. In Ceylon, the exorcist will demand the name of the demon possessing a demoniac, and the patient in frenzy answers, giving the demon's name, "I am So-and-So; I demand a human sacrifice, and I will not go without." The victim is promised, the patient comes to from the fit, and a few weeks later the sacrifice is made, but instead of a man they offer a fowl. Classic examples of a substitution of this sort may be found in the sacrifice of a doe for a virgin to Artemis in Laodicaea, a goat for a boy to Dionysos at Potniae. There appears to be a Semitic connection here, as there clearly is in the story of the Æolians of Tenedos sacrificing to Melikertes (Melkarth) instead of a new-born child a new-born calf, shoeing it with buskins and tending the mother cow as if a human mother.—("Primitive Culture," E. B. Tylor, London, 1871, vol. 2, p. 366; or in New York edition, 1879, vol. 2, pp. 403, 404.)

Inman takes the ground that the very same substitution occurred among the Hebrews. Commenting upon I Kings: xix, 18, he says:

In the Vulgate, the passage is thus rendered: "They say to these, 'Sacrifice the men who adore the calves;' while the Septuagint renders the words 'Sacrifice men, for the calves have come to an end,' indicating a reversion to human sacrifice."—(Inman, Ancient Faiths Embodied in Ancient Names, London, 1878, article "Hosea." Consult also Ragozin, "Assyria," New York, 1887, pp. 127, 128.)

---

*Dubois declares that in the Atharvana Veda "bloody sacrifices of victims (human not excepted) are there prescribed."—(Dubois, "People of India," London, 1817, p. 341.) And in those parts of India where human sacrifice had been abolished, a substitutive ceremony was practiced "by forming a human figure of flour paste or clay, which they carry into the temple and there cut off its head and mutilate it, in various ways, in presence of the idols."—(*Idem*, p. 190.)

If the cow have displaced a human victim, may it not be within the limits of probability that the ordure and urine of the sacred bovine are substitutes not only for the complete carcass, but that they symbolize a former use of human excreta?* The existence of ur-orgies has been indicated in Siberia, where the religion partakes of many of the characteristics of Buddhism. The minatory phraseology of the Brahminical inhibition of the use of the fungi which enter into these orgies has been given *verbatim;* so that, even did no better evidence exist, enough has been presented to open up a wide range of discussion as to the former area of distribution of loathsome and disgusting ceremonials which are now happily restricted to small and constantly diminishing zones.

HUMAN ORDURE AND URINE STILL USED IN INDIA.

It is well to remember, however, that in India the more generally recognized efficacy of cow urine and cow dung has not blinded the fanatical devotee to the necessity of occasionally having recourse to the human product.

At about ten leagues to the southward of Seringapatam there is a village called Nan-ja-na-gud, in which there is a temple famous all over the Mysore. Amongst the number of votaries of every caste who resort to it, a great proportion consists of barren women, who bring offerings to the god of the place, and pray for the gift of fruitfulness in return. But the object is not to be accomplished by the offerings and prayers alone, the disgusting part of the ceremony being still to follow. On retiring from the temple, the woman and her husband repair to the common sewer to which all the pilgrims resort in obedience to the calls of nature. There the husband and wife collect, with their hands, a quantity of the ordure, which they set apart, with a mark upon it, that it may not be touched by any one else; and with their fingers in this condition, they take the water of the sewer in the hollow of their hands and drink it. Then they perform ablution and retire. In two or three days they return to the place of filth, to visit the mass of ordure which they left. They turn it over with their hands, break it, and examine it in every possible way; and, if they find that any insects or vermin are engendered in it, they consider it a favorable prognostic for the woman.—(Abbé Dubois, "People of India," London, 1817, p. 411.†)

EXCREMENT GODS OF ROMANS AND EGYPTIANS.

The Romans and Egyptians went farther than this; they had gods of excrement, whose special function was the care of latrines and those who

* After the Jews had been humbled by the Lord and made to mingle *human* ordure with their bread, the punishment was mitigated by substitution. "Then he said unto me, Lo! I have given thee cow's dung for man's dung, and thou shalt prepare thy bread therewith."—(Ezekiel, iv: 15.)

† Previous notes upon the Grand Lama of Thibet and upon the abominable practices of the Agozis and Gurus seem to be pertinent in this connection. See page 17.

frequented them. Torquemada, a Spanish author of high repute, expresses this in very plain language:

I assert that they used *to adore* (as St. Clement writes to St. James the Less) stinking and filthy privies and water-closets; and, what is viler and yet more abominable, and an occasion for our tears and not to be borne with or so much as mentioned by name, they adored the noise and wind of the stomach when it expels from itself any cold or flatulence; and other things of the same kind, which, according to the same saint, it would be a shame to name or describe.*

In the preceding lines Torquemada refers to the Egyptians only, but, as will be seen by examining the Spanish notes below, his language is almost the same when speaking of the Romans.† The Roman goddess was called Cloacina. She was one of the first of the Roman deities, and is believed to have been named by Romulus himself. Under her charge were the various cloacæ, sewers, privies, &c., of the Eternal City.‡

ISRAELITISH DUNG GODS.

Dulaure quotes from a number of authorities to show that the Israelites and Moabites had the same ridiculous and disgusting ceremonial in their worship of Bel-phegor. The devotee presented his naked posterior before the altar and relieved his entrails, making an offering to the idol of the

---

*Digo que adoraban (segun San Clemente escrive á Santiago el menor), las hediondas y sucias necessarias y latrinas: y lo que es peor y mas abominable y digno de llorar y no de sufrir, ni nombrarle por su nombre, que adoraban, el estruendo y crugimiento, que hace el vientre quando despide de si alguna frialdad ó ventosidad y otras semejantes, que segun el mismo santo es verguënza nombrarlas y decirlas.—(Torquemada, Monarchia Indiana, lib. 6, chap. 13, Madrid, 1723.)

†Los Romanos * * * constituieron Diosa á los hediondas necesarias ó latrinas y la adoraban y consagraban y ofrecian sacrificios.—(Torquemada, Monarchia Indiana, lib. 6, chap. 16, Madrid, 1723.)

‡ There is another opinion concerning Cloacina—that she was one of the names given to a statue of Venus found in the Cloaca Maxima. Smith, in his Dictionary of Antiquities, London, 1850, expresses this view, and seems to be followed by the American and Britannic Encyclopædias. Lemprière defines Cloacina: "A goddess of Rome, who presided over the Cloacæ—some suppose her to be Venus—whose statue was found in the Cloacæ, whence the name." See, also, in Anthon's Classical Dictionary.

Higgins says that "the famous statue of Venus Cloacina was found in them (the Cloacæ Maximæ) by Romulus."—(Anacalypsis, foot-note to p. 624, London, 1836.)

Torquemada insists that the Romans borrowed this goddess from the Egyptians: "A esta diosa llamaron Cloacina, Diosa que presidia en sus albanares y los guardaba, que son los lugares donde van á parar todas las suciedades, inmundicias, y vascosidades de una Republica."—(Torquemada, lib. 6, chap. 17.)

Torquemada, who makes manifest in his writings an intimate acquaintance with Greek and Roman mythology, fortifies his position by references from St. Clement, Itinerar, lib. 5; Lactantius, Divinas Ejus, lib. 1, chap. 20; Epistle of St. Clement to St. James the Less, Eusebius, de Praeperatio Evangil., chap. 1; St. Augustine, Civ. Dei, lib. 2, chap. 22; Diod, Sic., lib. 1, chap. 2, and lib. 2, chap. 4; Lucian, Dialogues, Cicero, de Nat. Deorum, Pliny, lib. 10, chap. 27, and lib. 11, chap. 21; Theodoret, lib. 3, de Evangelii veritatis cognitione.

foul emanations.* Dung gods are also mentioned as having been known to the chosen people during the time of their idolatry.†

Besides Suchiquecal, the mother of the gods, who has been represented as eating excrement in token of humiliation, the Mexicans had other deities whose functions were more or less clearly complicated with alvine dejections. The most prominent of these was Ixcuina, called, also, Tlaçolteotl, of whom Brasseur de Bourbourg speaks in these terms:

> The goddess of ordure, or Tlaçolquani, the *eater of ordure*, because she presided over loves and carnal pleasures.‡

Mendieta mentions her as masculine, and in these terms:

> The god of vices and dirtinesses, whom they called Tlazulteotl.§

Bancroft speaks of "the Mexican goddess of carnal love, called Tlazoltecotl, Ixcuina, Tlacloquani," &c., and says that she—

> * * * had in her service a crowd of dwarfs, buffoons, and hunchbacks, who diverted her with their songs and dances and acted as messengers to such gods as she took a fancy to. The last name of this goddess means "eater of filthy things," referring, it is said, to her function of hearing and pardoning the confessions of men and women guilty of unclean and carnal crimes.—(Bancroft, H. H. Native Races of the Pacific Slope, vol. 3, p. 380.)

In the manuscript explaining the Codex Telleriano, given in Kingsborough's "Mexican Antiquities," vol. 5, p. 131, occurs the name of the goddess Ochpaniztli, whose feast fell on the 12th of September of our

---

* L'adorateur présentait devant l'autel son postérior nu, soulageait ses entrailles et faisait à l'idole une offrande de sa puante déjection.—(Dulaure, "Des Divinités Génératrices," Paris, 1825, p. 76.)

Philo says the devotee of Baal-Peor presented to the idol all the outward orifices of the body. Another authority says that the worshiper not only presented all these to the idol, but that the emanations or excretions were also presented—tears from the eyes, wax from the ears, pus from the nose, saliva from the mouth, and urine and dejecta from the lower openings. This was the god to which the Jews joined themselves; and these, in all probability, were the ceremonies they practiced in his worship.—(Robert Allen Campbell, Phallic Worship, St. Louis, 1888, p. 171.)

Still another authority says the worshiper, presenting his bare posterior to the altar, relieved his bowels, and offered the result to the idol: "Eo quod distendebant coram illo foramen podicis et stercus offerebant."—(Hargrave Jennings, Phallicism, London, 1884, quoting Rabbi Solomon Jarchi, in his Commentary on Numbers XXV.)

These two citations go to show that the worshiper intended making not a merely ceremonial offering of flatulence, but an actual oblation of excrement, such as has been stated, was placed upon the altars of their near neighbors, the Assyrians, in the devotions tendered their Venus.

† Ye have seen dung gods, wood and stone.—(Deut., xxix: 17. See Cruden's Concordance Articles, "Dung" and "Dungy," but no light is thrown upon the expression.)

And ye have seen their abominations and their idols (detestable things), wood and stone, silver and gold, which were among them.—(Lange's Commentary on Deuteronomy, edited by Dr. Philip Schaff, New York, 1879. But in foot-note one reads, "Margin—dungy gods from the shape of the ordure, literally thin clods or balls, or that which can be rolled about.—A. G.")

‡ Tlaçolteotl, la déese de l'ordure, ou Tlaçolquani, la mangeuse d'ordure, parcequ'elle présidait aux amours et aux plaisirs lubriques.—(Brasseur de Bourbourg, introduction to Landa, French edition, Paris, 1864, p. 87.)

§ El dios de los vicios y suciedades que le decian Tlazulteotl.—(Mendieta, in Icazbalceta, Mexico, 1870, vol. 1, p. 81.)

calendar. She was described as "the one who sinned by eating the fruit of the tree." The Spanish monks styled her, as well as another goddess, Tlaçolteotl—"La diosa de basura ó pecado." But "basura" is not the alternative of sin (pecado); it means "dung, manure, ordure, excrement."* It is possible that, in their zeal to discover analogies between the Aztec and Christian religions, the early missionaries passed over a number of points now left to conjecture.

In the same volume of Kingsborough, p. 136, there is an allusion to the offerings or sacrifices made Tepeololtec, "que, en romance, quiere decir sacrificios de mierda," which, "in plain language, signifies sacrifices of excrement." Nothing further can be adduced upon the subject, although a note at the foot of this page, in Kingsborough, says that here several pages of the Codex Telleriano had been obliterated or mutilated, probably by some over-zealous expurgator.

Knowing of the existence of "dung gods" among Romans, Egyptians, Hebrews, and Moabites, it is not unreasonable to insist, in the present case, upon a rigid adherence to the text, and to assert that, where it speaks of a sacrifice as a sacrifice of excrement and designates a deity as an eater of excrement, it means what it says, and should not be distorted, under the plea of symbolism, into a perversion of facts and ideas.

THE USE OF THE LINGAM IN INDIA.

Such a symbolism is to be detected in the use of the lingam in the East Indies, and it is a symbolism strikingly adapted to the intent of this article. In describing the sacrifice called Poojah, Maurice relates that—

> The Abichegam makes a part of the Pooja. This ceremony consists in pouring milk upon the lingam. This liquor is afterward kept with great care, and some drops are given to dying people that they may merit the delights of the Calaison.†

Again, he speaks of the salagram, a stone which is to the Vishnuite what the lingam is to the Seevites:

> Happy are those favored devotees who can quaff the sanctified water in which either has been bathed.‡

Dulaure describes the rites of the Cachi-couris, in which the sacred water of the Ganges is first poured upon the lingam; after flowing upon

*According to Neumann and Baretti's Velasquez, while, according to the dictionary of the Spanish Academy, the meaning is "the dirt and dust collected in sweeping—the sweepings and dung of stables."

†Maurice, "Indian Antiquities," London, 1800, vol. 5, p. 179.

‡*Idem*, p. 146.

the lingam, it is carefully preserved and dealt out in drops to the faithful. It is of special service in soothing the last hours of the dying.*

The lingam is the phallic symbol. The water or milk sanctified by it may represent a former employment of urine, such, as will soon be shown, prevailed all over Europe. This use of lingam water is perhaps analogous to that of mistletoe water, previously noted.

URINE AND ORDURE AS SIGNS OF MOURNING.

Care should be taken to distinguish between the religious use of ordure and urine and that in which they figure as outward signs of mourning, induced by a frenzy of grief, or where they have been utilized in the arts.

Lord Kingsborough (Mexican Antiquities, vol. 8, p. 237) briefly outlines such ritualistic defilement in the Mortuary Ceremonies of Hebrews and Aztecs, giving as references for the latter Diego Duran, and for the former the prophet Zechariah, chap. iii: "Now Joshua was clothed with filthy garments and stood before the angel," &c.

URINE AND ORDURE IN INDUSTRIES.

By the Eskimo urine is preserved for use in tanning skins,† while its employment in the preparation of leather in both Europe and America is too well understood to require any reference to authorities.

The Kioways of the Great Plains soaked their buffalo hides in urine to make them soft and flexible.‡

Bernal Diaz, in his enumeration of the articles for sale in the "tianguez" or market-places of Tenochtitlan, uses this expression:

> I must also mention human excrements which were exposed for sale in canoes lying in the canals near this square, which is used for the tanning of leather; for, according to the assurances of the Mexicans, it is impossible to tan well without it.—(Bernal Diaz, "Conquest of Mexico," London, 1844, vol. 1, p. 236.)

The same use of ordure in tanning bear-skins can be found among the nomadic Apaches of Arizona, although, preferentially, they use the ordure of the animal itself.

---

* Verser quelques gouttes sur la tête et dans la bouche des agonisants.—(Dulaure, "Des Divinités Génératrices," Paris, 1825, pp. 105, 106, 111.)

† They also keep urine in tubs in their huts for use in dressing deer and seal skins. (Hans Egede: also quoted in Richardson, "Polar Regions," Edinburgh, 1861, p. 304.) The same custom has been noted in Alaska. The same thing mentioned by Egede's grand nephew, Hans Egede Saabye. "Greenland," London, 1816, p. 6.

‡ The whole process was carefully observed by Captain Robert G. Carter, 4th Cavalry, U.S. Army.

Gómara, who also tabulated the articles sold in the Mexican markets, does not mention ordure in direct terms; his words are more vague:

All these things which I speak of, with many that I do not know and others about which I keep silent, are sold in this market of the Mexicans.*

Urine figures as the mordant for fixing the colors of blankets and other woolen fabrics woven by the Navajoes of New Mexico, by the Mokis of Arizona, by the Zunis and other Pueblos of the Southwest, by the Araucanians of Chile, by Mexicans, Peruvians, by some of the tribes of Afghanistan, and other nations; by all of whom it is carefully preserved. In the interior of China, travelers relate that copper receptacles along the roadsides rescue from loss a fertilizer whose value is fully recognized. In Germany and France, during the past century, farmers and gardeners were generally careful of this fertilizer.

"In the valley of Cuzco, Peru, and, indeed, in almost all parts of the Sierra, they used human manure for the maize crops, because they said it was the best." (Garcillasso de la Vega, "Comentarios Reales," Clement C. Markham's Translation, in Hakluyt Society, vol. 45, p. 11.)

Animal manure was known as a fertilizer to the Jews. (2 Kings, ix: 37. Jeremiah, viii: 2; ix: 22; xvi: 4; xxv: 33.)

Human manure also. (Consult McClintock and Strong's Encyclopædia, article, "Dung.")

Urine has also been employed as a detergent in scouring wool. (See Encyclopædia Britannica, article, "Bleaching.")

Diderot and D'Alembert say that the sal ammoniac of the ancients was prepared with the urine of camels; that phosphorus, as then manufactured in England, was made with human urine, as was also saltpeter. (Encyclopædia, Geneva, 1789, article "Urine.")

Sal ammoniac derives its name from having been first made in the vicinity of the temple of Jupiter Ammon; it would be of consequence to us to know whether or not the priests of that temple had administered urine in disease before they learned how to extract from it the medicinal salt which has come down to our own times.

The employment of different manures as fuel for firing pottery among Mokis, Zunis, and other Pueblos, and for general heating in Thibet, has been pointed out by the author in a former work. (Snake Dance of the Mokis, London, 1884; New York, 1884.) It was used for the same

* Todo estas cosas que digo y muchas que no sé y otras que callo, se venden en este mercado destos de Mejico.—(Gómara, "Historia de la Conquista de Mejico," p. 349.)

purpose in Africa, according to Mungo Park. (Travels, &c., p. 119.) The dung of the buffalo served the same purpose in the domestic economy of the Plains Indians. Camel dung is the fuel of the Bedouins; that of men and animals alike was saved and dried by the Syrians, Arabians, Egyptians, and people of West of England for fuel. Egyptians heated their lime-kilns with it. (McClintock and Strong, "Dung." See, also, Kitto's Biblical Encyclopædia, article "Dung.")

For shampooing the hair, it was the favorite medium among the Eskimo.*

Sahagun gives, in detail, the formula of the preparation applied by the Mexicans for the eradication of dandruff:

> Cut the hair close to root, wash head well with urine, and afterward take amole (soap-weed) and coixochitl leaves—the amole is the wormwood of this country [in this Sahagun is mistaken]—and then the kernels of aguacate ground up and mixed with the ashes already spoken of (wood ashes from the fire-place), and then rub on black mud with a quantity of the bark mentioned [mesquite].†

A similar method of dressing the hair, but without urine, prevails among the Indians along the Rio Colorado and in Sonora, Mexico. First, an application is made of a mixture of river mud ("blue mud," as it is called in Arizona) and pounded mesquite bark. After three days this is removed, and the hair thoroughly washed with water in which the saponaceous roots of the the amole have been steeped. The hair is dyed a rich blue-black, and remains soft, smooth, and glossy.

In the examples just given, as well as in a few to follow, where urine is applied in bodily ablutions, the object sought is undoubtedly the procuring of ammonia by oxidation; to none of these can any association of religious ideas be ascribed. Such will not be the case, however, where the ablutions are attended with ceremonial observances, are incorporated in a ritual, or take place in chambers reserved for sacred purposes. No difficulty is experienced in assigning to their proper categories the urinal ablutions of the Eskimo of Greenland,‡ of Alaska,§ of the northwest coast of America,‖ of the Indians of Cape Flattery,¶ of the people

---

* See Graah, "Greenland," London, 1837, p. 111, and Hans Egede Saabye, "Greenland," London, 1818, p. 256.

† Contra la caspa será necesario cortar muy á raiz los cabellos y lavarse la cabeza con orines y despues tomar las hojas de ciertas yerbas que en indio se llaman coioxochitl y amolli ó iztahuatl que es el agenjo de esta tierra, y con el cuesco del aguacate molido y mezclado con el cisco que está dicho arriba; y sobre esto se ha de poner, el barro negro que está referido, con cantidad de la corteza de lo dicho.—(Sahagun, in Kingsborough, vol. 7, p. 294.)

‡ Hans Egede Saabye, p. 256.

§ Sabytchew's Travels, in Phillips' Voyages, vol. 6, London, 1807.

‖ Whymper's Alaska, London, 1868, p. 142. Bancroft, H. H. Native Races Pacific Slope, vol. 1, p. 83.

¶ Swan, in Smithsonian Contributions, 1869, No. 220.

of Iceland,* and of the savages of Lower California,† or of the Celtiberii of Spain.

Although they boasted of cleanliness, both in their nourishment and in their dress, it was not unusual for them to wash their teeth and bodies in urine—a custom which they considered favorable to health.—(Maltebrun, Universal Geography, article, "Spain," vol. 5, book 137, p. 357, American edition, Philadelphia, 1832.)

This usage has been transmitted with some modification to the peasantry of Portugal, who are, partially at least, Celtiberian in blood. In some sections of Portugal, as is shown by Ivan Petroff, they wash their clothes in urine. ‡

URINE IN CEREMONIAL OBSERVANCES.

But in the examples adduced from Whymper concerning the people of the village of Unlacheet, on Norton Sound, "the *dancers* of the Malemutes of Norton Sound bathed themselves in urine." § Although, on another page, Whymper says that this was for want of soap, doubt may, with some reason, be entertained. Bathing is a frequent accompaniment, an integral part of the religious ceremonial among all the Indians of America, and no doubt among the Inuit or Eskimo as well; when this is performed by dancers, there is further reason to examine carefully for a religious complication, and especially if these dances be celebrated in sacred places, as Petroff relates they are.

They never bathe or wash their bodies, but on certain occasions the men light a fire in the kashima, strip themselves, and dance and jump around until in a profuse perspiration. They then apply urine to their oily bodies and rub themselves until a lather appears, after which they plunge into the river.‖

In each village of the Kuskutchewak (of Alaska) there is a public building named the kashim, in which councils are held and festivals kept, and which must be large enough

* "People of Iceland were reported to wash their hands and their faces in pisse." (Hakluyt, Voyages, vol. 1, p. 664.) This report, however, was indignantly denied of all but the common people, by Arugrianus Jonas, an Icelandic writer.

† Pericuis of Lower California, "Mothers, to protect them against the weather, cover the entire bodies of their children with a varnish of coal and urine."—(Bancroft, *idem*, vol. 1, p. 559.)

Clavigero not only tells all that Bancroft does, but he adds that the women of California washed their own faces in urine.—(Historia de Baja California, Mexico, 1852, p. 28.)

‡ Ivan Petroff in "Transactions American Anthropological Society," vol. 1, 1882.

Clavigero quotes Diodorus Siculus to the effect that the Celtiberians bathed in urine and cleaned their teeth with it. "Urina totum corpus perluunt, adeoque dentes etiam fricant."—(Diod. Siculus, lib. 5, in Clavigero, Historia de Baja California, Mexico, 1852, p. 28.)

Diderot and D'Alembert assert unequivocally that in the later years of the last century the people of the Spanish Peninsula still used urine as a dentifrice.

Les Espagnols font grand usage de l'urine pour se nettoyer les dents. Les anciens Celtibériens faisoient la même chose.—(Encyclopædia, Geneva, 1789, article "Urine.")

§ Whymper's "Alaska," London, 1868, pp. 142, 152.

‖ Ivan Petroff in "Transactions American Anthropological Society," vol. 1, 1882.

to contain all the grown men of the village. It has raised platforms around the walls and a place in the center for a fire, with an aperture in the roof for the admission of light.—(Richardson, Arctic Searching Expedition, London, 1851, p. 365.)

These kashima are identical with the estufas of Zunis, Moquis, and Rio Grande Pueblos. Whymper himself describes them thus:

These buildings may be regarded as the natives' town hall; orations are made, festivals and feasts are held in them.

No room is left for doubt after reading the fuller description of these Kashima, contained in Bancroft. He says that the Eskimo dance in them, "often in puris naturalibus," and make "burlesque imitations of birds and beasts." Dog or wolf tails hang to the rear of their garments. A sacred feast of fish and berries accompanies these dances, wherein the actors "elevate the provisions successively to the four cardinal points and once to the skies above, when all partake of the feast."*

ORDURE IN SMOKING.

Among all the observances of the every-day life of the American aborigines, none is so distinctly complicated with the religious idea as smoking; therefore, should the use of excrement, human or animal, be detected in this connection, full play should be given to the suspicion that a hidden meaning attaches to the ceremony. This would appear to be the view entertained by the indefatigable missionary, De Smet, who records such a custom among the Flatheads and Crows in 1846:

To render the odor of the pacific incense agreeable to their gods it is necessary that the tobacco and the herb (skwiltz), the usual ingredients, should be mixed with a small quantity of buffalo dung.†

The Sioux, Cheyennes, Arapahoes, and others of the plains tribes, to whom the buffalo is a god, have the same or an almost similar custom.

* Bancroft, H. H. Native Races Pacific Slope, vol. 1, p. 75.

† Father De Smet, "Oregon Missions," New York, 1847, p. 383.

The Peruvians had one class of "wizards" (*i. e.*, medicine men), who "told fortunes by maize and the dung of sheep." (Fables and Rites of the Yncas, Padre Cristoval de Molina, translated by Clement C. Markham, Hakluyt Society Transactions, London, 1873, vol. 48, p. 14.) Molina resided in Cuzco, as a missionary, from 1570 to 1584.

Les Hachus (a division of the Peruvian priesthood), consultaient l'avenir au moyen de grains de mäis ou des excrements des animaux.—(Balboa, Histoire de Pérou, p. 29, in Ternaux, vol. 15.)

See, also, D. G. Brinton's "Myths of the New World," New York, 1868, pp. 278, 279.

Ducange, enumerating the pagan superstitions which still survived in Europe in A. D. 743, mentions divination or augury by the dung of horses, cattle, or birds.

Del auguriis vel avium, vel equorum, vel boum stercoracibus.—(Ducange, Glossary, article "Stercoraces.")

ORDURE AND URINE IN MEDICINE.

The administration of urine as a curative opens the door to a flood of thought. Medicine, both in theory and practice, even among nations of the highest development and refinement, has not, until within the present century, cleared its skirts of the superstitious hand-prints of the dark ages. With tribes of a lower degree of culture it is still subordinate to the incantations and exorcisms of the "medicine man." It might not be going a step too far to assert that the science of therapeutics, pure and simple, has not yet taken form among savages; but to shorten discussion and avoid controversy, it will be assumed here that such a science does exist, but in an extremely rude and embryotic state; and to this can be referred all examples of the introduction of urine or ordure in the *materia medica*, where the aid of the "medicine man" does not seem to have been invoked, as in the method employed for the eradication of dandruff by Mexicans, Eskimo, and others, the Celtiberian dentrifice, &c.*

The Indians of California gave urine to newly-born children. "At time of childbirth many singular observances obtained; for instance, the old women washed the child as soon as it was born and drank of the water; the unhappy infant was forced to take a draught of urine, medicinally."†

So in Peru, "when sucking infants were taken ill, especially if their ailment was of a feverish nature, they washed them in urine in the mornings, and when they could get some of the urine of the child they gave it a drink."‡

Ignorant people in both Europe and America have been accused of nearly identical vagaries in domestic medicine.

Along the Isthmus of Darien the belief was prevalent among the aborigines that the most efficacious remedy for poisoned arrows was that which required the wounded man to swallow pills of his own excrement.§

Padre Inamma, whose interesting researches upon rattlesnake bites and their remedies (made in Lower California, some time before the ex-

* Mungo Park states that he saw it applied as a poultice for suppurating abscesses among Mandingoes. (Travels in Africa, New York, &c., p. 203.) The author has seen it plastered upon bee-stings, with a soothing effect, in New Jersey.

† Bancroft, H. H. Native Races, vol. 1, p. 413.

‡ Garcilasso de la Vega, Comentarios Reales, Markham's Translation, Hakluyt Society, vol. 41, p. 186.

§ Decian que era el antidoto de esta ponçona el Fuego i el agua del mar, la dieta y continencia. Y otra dicen que la hez del herido tomada en pildoras o en otra forma. (Herrera, Decades, 2, lib. 1, pp. 3, 9, 10.) They used to say that the antidotes for this poison were fire, sea-water, fasting, and continence. Another of which they speak was the excrement of the wounded man taken in form of pill or otherwise.

pulsion of the Jesuits, in 1767) are published in Clavigero,* says that the most usual and most efficacious antidote was human ordure, fresh and dissolved in water, drunk by the person bitten.

Analogous medicaments may be hinted at in Smith's account of the Aracuanians of Chile:

Their remedies are principally, if not entirely, vegetable matter, though they administer many disgusting compounds of animal matter, which they pretend are endowed with miraculous powers.—(Smith, Araucauians, New York, 1855, p. 234.)

Brand enumerates obsolete recipes, one of which (disease not mentioned) directed the patient to take "five spoonfuls of knave child urine of an innocent." †

The Siberians gave human urine to their reindeer:

Nothing is so acceptable to a reindeer as human urine, and I have even seen them run to get it as occasion offered.—(John Dundas Cochrane, Pedestrian Journey Through Siberian Tartary, 1820–23, Philadelphia, 1824, p. 235.)

Here the intent was evident; the animals needed salt, and no other method of obtaining it was feasible during the winter months. Cochrane is speaking of the Tchuktchi, but he was also among Yakuts and other tribes. He walked from Saint Petersburgh to Kamtschatka and from point to point in Siberia for a total distance of over six thousand miles. His pages are dark with censure of the filthy and disgusting habits of the savage nomads, as, of the Yakuts, "their stench and filth are inconceivable." "The large tents (of the Tchuktchi) were disgustingly dirty and offensive, exhibiting every species of grossness and indelicacy." Inside the tents men, women, and girls were absolutely naked. "They drink only snow-water during the winter, to melt which, when no wood can be had, very disgusting and dirty means are resorted to," &c. But nowhere does he speak of the drinking of human urine, which, as has been learned from other sources, does obtain among them.

Thus far, the citations have not specifically mentioned the association of occult influence with human excreta, but those to follow impute, without vagueness or ambiguity, a mysterious and inexplicable potency to both urine and ordure.

* El remedio mas usual y eficaz es el de la triaca humana, asi llamada, para mayor decencia, el excremento humano, fresco y disuelto en aqua que hacen beber al mordido.—(Clavigero, Historia de la Baja California, Mexico, 1852.)

† Brand, Popular Antiquities, London, 1849, vol. 3, p. 282.

OCCULT INFLUENCES ASCRIBED TO ORDURE AND URINE.

In Canada, human urine was drunk as a medicine. Father Sagard witnessed a dance of the Hurons in which the young men, women, and girls danced naked around a sick woman, into whose mouth one of the young men urinated, she swallowing the disgusting draught in the hope of being cured.*

By the French, it was considered a certain cure for fever. Such an amount of superstition attached to the panacea that the prescription may well be given in full:

> Knead a small loaf with urine voided in the worst stage of his fever by a person having the quaternary ague. Bake the loaf, let it cool, and give it to be eaten by another person. Repeat the same during three different attacks, and the fever will leave the patient and go to the person who has eaten the bread.

Another one runs in these terms:

> Take an egg, boil it hard, and break off the shell. Prick the egg in different places with a needle, steep it in the urine of a person afflicted with fever, and then give it to a man (if the patient be a man), to a woman (if a woman), and the recipient will acquire the fever, which will abandon the patient.†

This remedy Thiers traces back to the Romans, quoting from Horace in support of his assertion.

The second recipe finds its parallel in the "Chinook olives," described in the first pages of this monograph.

English women, in some localities, drank the urine of their husbands to assist them in the hour of labor.‡

---

* Il se fit un jour une dance de tous les jeunes hommes, femmes et filles toutes nues, en la présence d'une malade, à la quelle il fallut (traict que je ne sçay commen excuser ou passer sous silence), qu'un de ces jeunes hommes luy pissast dans la bouche et qu'elle auallast et beust cette eau, ce qu'elle fit avec un grand courage, esperant en receuoir guérison.—(Sagard, Histoire du Canada, edition of Paris, 1885, p. 107.)

† Pétrir un petit pain avec l'urine qu'une personne malade de la fièvre quarte aura rendue dans le fort de son accès, le faire cuire, le laisser froidir, le donner à manger à un * * * et faire trois fois la même chose pendant trois accès, le * * * prendra la fièvre quarte et elle quittera la personne malade.

Faire durcir un oeuf, le peler, le piquer de divers coups d'aiguille, le tremper dans l'urine d'une personne qui a la fièvre * * * puis le donner à un * * * si le malade est un mâle ou à une * * * si le malade est une femelle et la fièvre s'en ira.—(Thiers, Traité des Superstitions, Paris, 1745, vol. 1, lib. 5, cap. 4, p. 386. Copied in Picart, Coûtumes et Cérémonies, &c., Amsterdam, 1729, vol. 10, p. 80.)

‡ "In the collection entitled Sylon, or the Wood, p. 130, we read that 'a few years ago, in this same village, the women in labor used to drinke the urine of their husbands, who were all the while stationed, as I have seen the cows in St. James' Park, straining themselves to give as much as they can.'"—(Brand, Popular Antiquities, London, 1849, vol. 3, article, "Lady in the Straw.")

By the Irish peasantry, it was sprinkled upon sick children.*

American boys urinate upon their legs to prevent cramp while swimming.

By the Hottentot priests, it is said to have been sprinkled upon newly-married couples.†

FEARFUL RITE OF THE HOTTENTOTS.

A religious rite of still more fearful import occurs among the same people at the initiation of their young men into the rank of warriors—a ceremony which must be deferred until the postulant has attained his eighth or ninth year. It consists, principally, in depriving him of the left testicle, after which the medicine man voids his urine upon him.‡

With equal solicitude does the Hottentot medicine man follow the remains of his kinsmen to the grave, aspersing with the same sacred liquid the corpse of the dead and the persons of the mourners who bewail his loss.§

The French attributed to it other virtues beyond its efficacy as a febrifuge.

URINE USED TO DEFEAT WITCHCRAFT.

It was in requisition to ward off the machinations of witches. In the valuable compilation of superstitious practices interdicted by Roman Catholic councils Thiers includes the persons who bathe their hands with urine in the morning to avert witchcraft or nullify its effect. He says,

---

* Brand quotes Camden, as relating of the Irish, that "if a child is at any time out of order, they sprinkle it with the stalest urine they can get."—(Brand, Popular Antiquities, article "Christening Customs," London, 1849, vol. 2, p. 86.)

After the first portion of this monograph had gone to press, the author was fortunate in obtaining a copy of the recently published address of Mr. James Mooney, of the Bureau of Ethnology, Washington, D. C., upon the "Medical Mythology of Ireland."

This interesting and extremely valuable contribution, which can be found in the Transactions of the American Philosophical Society for 1887, leaves no uncertainty in regard to the mystic powers ascribed by the Celtic peasantry to both urine and ordure. Urine and *chicken dung* are shown to be potent in frustrating the mischief of fairies; "fire, iron, and dung," are spoken of as the "three great safeguards against the influence of fairies and the infernal spirits." Dung is carried about the person, as part of the contents of amulets; and children suffering from convulsions are, as a last resort, bathed from head to foot in urine, to rescue them from the clutches of their fairy persecutors.

† Mungo Park's Travels in Africa, New York, 1813, p. 109; also previous citation.

‡ See in Picart, Coûtumes et Cérémonies Réligieuses, etc., Réligion des Africains, Amsterdam, 1729, vol. 7, p. 47.)

§ Picart, Coûtumes et Cérémonies Réligieuses, etc., Amsterdam, 1729, vol. 7, pp. 52, 57.

too, that Saint Lucy was reputed to be a witch, for which reason the Roman judge, Paschasius, at her trial sprinkled her with urine.*

There is on record the confession of a young French witch, Jeanne Bosdean, at Bordeaux, 1594, wherein is described a witches' mass, at which the devil appeared in the disguise of a black buck, with a candle between his horns. When holy water was needed, the buck urinated in a hole in the ground, and the officiating witch aspersed it upon the congregation with a black sprinkler. Jeanne Bosdean adhered to her story even when in the flames.†

Leaving the continent and crossing the channel, the same queer usages, based upon the same ideas, are to be discovered. In England "it was a supposed remedy against witchcraft to put some of the bewitched person's water, with a quantity of pins, needles, and nails, into a bottle, cork them up, and set them before the fire, in order to confine the spirit."‡

At the trials of witches one of the usual tests was "the burning of the dung or urine of such as are bewitched."‡

For the detection of witches, "a handful of thatch from over the door, or a tile, if it be tiled," was taken from the suspected witch's house; "if it be thatch, you must wet and sprinkle it over with the patient's water, and likewise with salt."‡

There are several tests and remedies of the same general nature. It is believed that the foregoing will suffice. Brand says that the one last given was in vogue in Somersetshire as late as 1730.

"Pennant tells us that the Highlanders on New Year's Day burn juniper before their cattle, and on the first Monday in every quarter sprinkle them with urine.§

"Casting urine" is mentioned among the list of "superstitious practices preserved in the life and character of Harvey, the famous conjurer of Dublin, 1728."||

---

* Ceux qui lavent leurs mains le matin avec de l'urine pour détourner les maléfices ou pour en empecher l'effet. C'est pour cela que le juge Paschase fit arroser d'urine Sainte Luce, parce qu'il s'imaginoit qu'elle étoit sorcière.—(Thiers, Traité des Superstitions, Paris, 1741, vol. 1, cap. 5, p. 171.)

This statement is repeated verbatim by Picart (Coûtumes et Cérémonies, etc., Amsterdam, 1729, vol. 10, p. 35), and he adds, that the judge believed that he would by this precaution disable her from evading the torments in store for her. John of Saulsbury, bishop of Chartres, with good reason cast ridicule upon this charm.

† Pour faire de l'eau fénite, le Bouc pissoit dans un trou à terre et celui qui faisoit l'office en arrosoit les assistans avec un asperge noir.—(Thiers, Superstitions, etc., vol. 2, book 4, cap. 1, p. 367. See the same story in Picart, vol. 8, p. 69.)

‡ Brand's Popular Antiquities, London, 1849, vol. 3, pp. 13, 21, 25, 35.

§ Brand, Popular Antiquities, London, 1849, vol. 1, p. 13.

|| Brand, vol. 3, p. 170.

"Ostanes, the magician, prescribed the dipping of our feet, in the morning, in human urine as a preventative against charms."*

The malevolence of witchcraft seems to have taken its greatest pleasure in subtle assaults upon those just entering the married state. Fortunately, amulets, talismans, and counter charms were within reach of all who needed them; one of those only will be given—urination through the wedding ring.†

The Romans had a feast to the mother of all the gods, Berecinthia, in which the matrons took her idol and sprinkled it with their urine.‡

Berecinthia was one of the names under which Cybele or Rhea, the primal earth goddess, was worshiped by the Romans and by many nations in the East. Her priests, the Galli, emasculated themselves in orgies whose frenzy was of the same general type as the Omophagi of the Greeks, previously described.

It is strange to encounter in races so diverse apparently as the Greeks and the Hottentots the same rites of emasculation and urine sprinkling.

Father Le Jeune must have been on the track of something corresponding to an ur-orgie among the Hurons when he learned that the devil imposed upon the sick, in dreams, the duty of wallowing in ordure if they hoped for restoration to health.§

The following is described as the Abyssinian method of exorcising a woman: The exorcist "lays an amulet on the patient's heaving bosom. makes her smell of some vile compound, and the moment her madness is somewhat abated begins a dialogue with the Bouda (demon), who answers in a woman's voice. The devil is invited to come out in the name of all the saints, but a threat to treat him with some red hot coals is usually more potent, and after he has promised to obey, he seeks to delay his exit by asking for something to eat. *Filth and dirt* are mixed and hidden under a bush, when the woman crawls to the sickening repast and gulps it down with avidity." (From an article entitled "Abyssinian Women," in the "Evening Star," Washington, D. C., October 17, 1885.)

ORDURE IN LOVE-PHILTERS.

Love-sick maidens in France stand accused of making as a philter a cake, into whose composition entered "nameless ingredients," which con-

* Brand, vol. 3, p. 286.

† * * * through the wedding ring.—(Brand, vol. 3, p. 305.)

‡ La rociaba con sus orines.—(Torquemada, Monarchia Indiana, lib. x, chap. xxiii.)

§ Leur faisant voir en songe, qu'ils ne sçauroient guerir qu'en se veautant dans toutes sortes d'ordures.—(Pére Le Jeune, Jesuit Relations, 1636. Published by Canadian Government, Quebec, 1858.)

fection being eaten by the refractory lover, soon caused a revival of his waning affections.* This was considered to savor so strongly of witchcraft that it was interdicted by councils.

The witches and wizards of the Apache tribe make a confection or philter one of the ingredients of which is generally human ordure, as the author learned from some of them a few years since. The Navajoes, of same blood and language as the Apaches, employ the dung of cows (as related in the "Snake Dance of the Mokis," p. 75).

This recapitulation of urinal aspersions, ablutions, &c., is sufficient to expose the very widespread dissemination of the rite, which in the case of the European races at least may be referred to an origin in India in the earliest ages of the human family. The resemblances cannot safely be explained away as accidental; the Aryan tribes, in their migrations from the far East, took with them languages, religious rites and ceremonies, and social usages whose counterpart, slightly altered or distorted perhaps in transmission, may be stumbled upon among distantly related brethren in the former habitat.

The love-philter described in the preceding paragraph recalls a somewhat analogous practice among the Manicheans, whose eucharistic bread was incorporated or sprinkled with human semen, possibly with the idea that the bread of life should be strengthened by the life-giving excretion.†

The Albigenses, or Catharistes, their descendants, are alleged to have degenerated into or to have preserved the same vile superstition.‡

Understanding that these allegations proceed from hostile sources, their insertion in this category has been permitted only upon the theory that as the Manichean ethics and ritual present resemblances to both the

*"Le maléfice amoureux ou le philtre" is defined as follows: "Telle est la pratique de certaines femmes et de certaines filles qui, pour obliger leurs galans * * * de les aimer comme auparavant * * * les font manger du gateau où elles ont mis des ordures que je ne veux pas nommer."—(Jean Baptiste Thiers, Traité des Superstitions," Paris, 1741, p. 150.)

†Quâ occasione vel potius execrabilis superstitionis quadam necessitate coguntur electi eorum velut eucharistiam conspersam cum semine humano sumere.—(Saint Augustine, quoted by Bayle, Philosophical Dictionary, English edition, London, 1737, article "Manicheans.")

‡Les Catharistes qui étoient une espèce choisis de Manichéens, pétrissoient le pain Eucharistique avec la sémence humaine.—(Thiers, Superstitions, &c., Paris, 1741, vol. 2, lib. 2, chap. 1, p. 216; and Picart, Coutûmes et Cérémonies, &c., Amsterdam, 1729, vol. 8, p. 79.)

E. B. Tylor says that "about A. D. 700 John of Osun, patriarch of Armenia, wrote a diatribe against the sect of Paulicians" (who were believed to be the descendants of the Manicheans, and in turn to have transmitted their doctrines to the Albigenses). In the course of the diatribe the patriarch declares that "they mix wheaten flour with the blood of infants and therewith celebrate their communion."—(E. B. Tylor, Primitive Culture, London, 1871, vol. 1, p. 69.)

Parsee and Buddhist religions (from which they may to some extent have originated), there is reason for supposing that ritualistic ablutions, aspersions, and other practices analogous to those of the great sect farther to the East, may have been transmitted to the younger religion in Europe.*

BURLESQUE SURVIVALS.

A new task now presents itself—the examination into burlesque survivals of rites and usages no longer countenanced as matters of religious importance.

The Hindu festival of Holi, Huli, or Hulica, familiar to most readers, has thus been outlined by a recent witness as celebrated in the provinces near Oudeypore.† The proceedings are characterized as a saturnalia, attended with much freedom and excessive drunkenness:

From the very beginning, effigies of the most revolting indecency are set up in the gates of the town and in the principal thoroughfares.

Troops of men and women, wreathed with flowers and drunk with bang, crowd the streets, carrying sacks full of a bright red vegetable powder. With this they assail the passers-by, covering them with clouds of dust, which soon dyes their clothes a startling color. Groups of people stationed at the windows retaliate with thé same projectile, or squirt with *wooden syringes red and yellow streams of water into the streets below.*

The Nautch dances reach the acme of voluptuousness, and the accompanying chants are filled with suggestiveness. The author here quoted says that Holica was the Indian Venus.

An eminent authority says that—

This red powder (gulál) is a sign of a bad design of an adulterous character. During the holi holidays the Maharaj throws gulál on the breasts of female and male devotees, and directs the current of some water of a yellow color from a syringe upon the breasts of females.‡

This "yellow water" may be a survival of and a refinement upon urine. The Apaches and Navajoes, close neighbors of the Zunis, have had, until very recently (and may still celebrate), the Dance of the Joshkân, in which clowns scatter upon the spectators, from bladders wound round their bodies, water, said to be representative of urine.

*Manicheans bathed in urine.—(Picart, Coûtumes, &c., Dissertation sur les Perses, p. 18.)

†See in Rousselet's "India," London, 1876, pp. 173, 343. It has been identified as our April Fool's Day. See in "Asiatic Researches," Calcutta, 1790, vol. 2, p. 334; also, in Moor's "Hindu Pantheon," London, 1810, pp. 156, 157; also, the Encyclopædia Britannica, and Appleton's Encyclopædia, article "April."

On the Sunday and Monday preceding Lent people are privileged at Lisbon to play the fool; it is thought very jocose to *pour water* on any person who passes or *throw powder* in his face; but to do both is the perfection of wit.—(Southey, quoted in Hone's Every Day Book, vol. 1, p. 206, London, 1825. See Brand's Popular Antiquities, London, 1849, vol. 1, p. 131, article "April Fool's Day.")

‡ Inman, Ancient Faiths Embodied in Ancient Names, p. 393.

Among the Aztecs there was a festival allowing the fullest license to clowns, armed with bladders, filled with red powder or fine pieces of maguey paper, attached by strings to short poles. With these bladders all persons caught in the streets, especially women and girls, were mercilessly buffeted. (Sahagun, vol. 2, in Kingsborough's Mexican Antiquities, vol. 6, p. 33, and again, vol. 7, p. 83.)

His account says that in the seventeenth month, which was called Tititl, and corresponded almost to our winter solstice, the Mexican year being divided into eighteen months, of twenty days each, beginning with our February, the Aztec populace played a game called "nechichiquavilo."

All the men and boys who wished to play this game made little bags or nets, filled with the pollen of the rush, called espadaña, or with paper cut in fine pieces. These were attached to cords or ribbons half a yard long, in such a manner that a blow could be struck with them. Others made these bags like gloves, which they stuffed as above stated, or with leaves of green maize. No one was allowed, under penalty, to put into these bags any stones, or anything else which could hurt.

The boys at once began to play this game, in the way of a sham-battle, hitting each other on the head, or wherever else they could. As the fun increased, the more mischievous of the boys began to beat the young maidens passing along the street; at times, three or four young boys would attack one girl, and beat her so hard as to weary her and make her cry. The more prudent of the young girls, in going from point to point, carried a club with which to defend themselves. Some of the boys concealed the bag, and when any old women carelessly approached, they would suddenly begin to beat them, crying out "Chichiquatzinte mantze," which means "Our mother, this is the bag of the game." *

* Para este juego, todos los hombres y muchachos que querian jugar hacian taleguillas ó redecillos llenos de flor de las espadañas ó de algunos papeles rotos; ataban estos con unos cordelejos ó cintas de media vara de largo, de tal manera que pudiese hacer golpe; otros hacian á manera de guantes las taleguillas é hinchabanlos de lo arriba dicho ó de ojas de maiz verde; ponian pena á todos estos que nadie echase piedra ó cosa que pudiese lastimar dentro las taleguillos. Comenzaban luego los muchachos á jugar este juego á manera de escaramuza y dabanse de talegazos en la cabeza y por donde acertaban y de poco en poco se iban multiplicando de los muchachos y los mas traviesos daban de talegazos á las muchachos que pasaban por la calle: á las veces, se juntaban tres ó quatro para dar á una de tal manera que la fatigaban y la hacian llorar.

Algunos muchachas que eran mas discretas, si habian de ir á alguna parte, entonces llevaban un palo ú otra cosa que hiciese temer para defenderse. Algunos muchachos escondian la talega y quando pasaba alguna mujer descuidadamente, dabanla de talegazos y quando la daban un golpe, decian Chichiquatzinto mantze, que quiere decir "Madre Nuestra, és la talega de este juego." Las mugeres andaban muy recatadas quando ivan á alguna parte.—(Sahagun, in Kingsborough, vol 7, p. 83.)

At the feast of the goddess Tona the same game was played.—(See Sahagun, in Kingsborough, vol. 6, p. 33.)

The following is Torquemada's description:

> In the festival in honor of the goddess Yamatecuhtli, or "principal old woman," in the seventeenth month of the Mexican calendar, all the people of the city made bags after the manner of purses, and stuffed them full of hay and straw and other things which would have no weight and do no harm, and, attaching them to a cord, carried them hidden under their cloaks. With these bags they buffeted all the women they met on the streets.—(Torquemada, Monarchia Indiana, lib. 10, cap. 29.)

He recognizes the similarity between this and the blind-man's-buff games of other countries.*

A contributor to Asiatic Researches calls this powder of the Huli festival a "purple powder," and claims that the idea is to represent the return of spring, which the Romans called "purple."†

In the report of one of the early American explorations to the Trans-Missouri region occurs the story that the Republican Pawnees, Nebraska, once (about 1780–'90) violated the laws of hospitality by seizing a calumet-bearer of the Omahas who had entered their village, and, among other indignities, making him "drink urine mixed with bison gall." ‡

Bison gall itself sprinkled upon raw liver, just warm from the carcass, was regarded as a delicacy. The expression "excrement eater" is applied by the Mandans and others on the Upper Missouri as a term of the vilest opprobrium, according to Surgeon Washington Matthews, § U. S. Army, whose remarks are based upon an unusually extended and intelligent experience.

Doctor Garrett mentions "water of amber made by Paracelsus out of cow dung," and gives the recipe for its distillation, as well as for that of its near relative, "water of dung," the formula for which begins with the words, "Take of any kind of dung you please." ||

It is not beyond the limit of probability that in these obsolete medicaments flicker the dying flame of the idea still governing the Hindu woman craving the joys of maternity.

PHALLIC SUPERSTITIONS IN FRANCE.

And in like manner, as has already been shown of the sacred character attaching among the people of the far East to water, wine, or milk which

* Hacia toda la gente de el Pueblo unas talegas, á manera de bolsas, y henchianles de heno y paja y otras cosas que no hacen golpe ni tienen peso y colgavanlas de un cordel y traianlas escondidas debaio de las mantos que les servian de capas. Con estos talegas daban de Talegaços á todas las mugeres que encontraban por las colles.

† R. Patterson, in Asiatic Researches, Calcutta, 1805, vol. 8, p. 78.

‡ Long's Expedition, Philadelphia, 1823, vol. 1. p. 300.

§ Author of "Hidatsa," and other ethnological works of authority.

|| Garrett, Myths in Medicine, New York, 1881, pp. 148, 149.

had been poured over the lingam, the women of France solaced themselves with the hope that children would come to those who drank an infusion containing scrapings from the phalli, existing until the outbreak of the French revolution, at Puy en Velay, in the church of Saint Foutin; in the shrine of Saint Guerlichon, near Bruges; in the shrine of Guignolles, near Brest; and in that of an ancient statue of Priapus, at Antwerp.*

CONCLUDING REMARKS.

The resemblance to the customs of the East Indies was, in places, even closer than as above indicated.

Inman tells of sterile women who drank "priapic wine," *i. e.*, wine poured upon an upright conical stone representing the lingam, and then collected and allowed to turn sour. (Inman, "Ancient Faiths," &c., vol. 1, p. 305, article "Asher.")

The same statement is to be found in Hargrave Jennings' work, "Phallicism," London, 1884, p. 256, but it seems to be repeated from Inman and Dulaure. Campbell reports that "among the principal relics of the church at Embrun was the statue of Saint Foutin. The worshipers of this idol poured libations of wine upon its extremity, which was reddened by the practice. This wine was caught in a jar and allowed to turn sour. It was then called 'holy vinegar,' and was used by the women as a lotion with which to anoint the yoni." ("Phallic Worship," Robert Allen Campbell, St. Louis, Mo., 1888, p. 197.)

MEDICINAL EFFECTS OF URINE.

The fullest examination possible has been made of encyclopædias and medical works to ascertain the effects upon the human system of urine swallowed or absorbed. The only discovery has been in the work of

---

* See Dulaure's "Des Divinités Génératrices," Paris, 1825, pp. 271, 277, 278, 280, and 283. He says that this vestige of phallic worship was discernible in France "à une époque très-rapprochée de la nôtre," and that women "raclaient une énorme branche phallique que présentait la statue du saint; elles croyaient que la raclure enfusée dans un boisson, les rendrait fécondes."

But Davenport, who has probed deeply into the question of phallic worship, contends that such vestiges existed in some of the communities of France, Sicily, and Belgium, not only down to the Reformation, but even to the opening decades of the 19th century. (See Davenport "On the Powers of Reproduction," London (privately printed), 1869, pp. 10–20.)

E. Payne Knight speaks of this same instance of survival at Isernia, in Sicily. It was known at that place as late as 1805.

See, also, "The Masculine Cross and Ancient Sex Worship," Sha Rocco, New York, 1874, &c.

Dulaure, however, admits that he knew of no example in antiquity of scraping the phallus and drinking an infusion of the powder. "L'usage de racler le phallus et d'avaler de cette raclure avec de l'eau, usage dont je ne connais point d'exemple dans l'antiquité."

Dulaure, as above, p. 300.

Surgeon General Hammond, U. S. Army.* A chapter is devoted to uraemic intoxication or the exhilaration produced by the entrance into the blood of urine, either injected or abnormally absorbed. This part of the subject should be carefully scrutinized by medical experts, whose determinations may make known whether or not the drunken frenzy of the Zuni dancers could be attributed to the unnatural beverage exclusively or to that in combination with other intoxicants.

Only such matter has been admitted into this monograph as could *prima facie* be considered as having the right of entry; the greatest care has been taken to avoid distortion or mutilation of authorities, and much has been excluded that might have been presented without running a risk of being accused of unfairness.

For example, as old an authority as John de Laet calls attention to the great prevalence of intoxication and debauchery among the Indians of Vextipa, near Mexico, who on feast days had the ancient custom of becoming drunk as beasts and committing enormous excesses.† And in like manner the first missionaries in Canada complained of the brutal orgies of the natives, in which, under cover of darkness and the cloak of their superstitions, deeds were committed which the pen dared not describe. Ample reference to these has been preserved in the Jesuit relations, and in the exact and interesting American treatises dependent so largely upon them.‡ It is more likely, however, that the Huron and Algonkin saturnalia were, in general terms, scenes of promiscuous licentiousness.

Only two authorities can be cited, Fathers Le Jeune and Sagard, who instance the use of human urine or ordure under spiritual direction; all others leave the inference, that the bacchanalia of which they were the reluctant and disgusted observers had no other peculiarity than that of unrestrained sexual intercourse.

To confirm the testimony previously submitted upon the phallic origin of the custom of kissing under the mistletoe, the deductions of a recent

---

*Physiological Memoirs, New York, 1863.

Dunglison says: "Human urine was at one time considered aperient; and was given in jaundice in the dose of one or two ounces. Cow's urine, urina vaccae, all-flower water, was once used warm from the cow as a purge."—(Dunglison's Medical Dictionary, Philadelphia, Pa., 1860, article "Urine.")

†John de Laet, lib. vi, chap. vii, p. 202.

‡See Francis Parkman's "Jesuits in North America," the works of John Gilmary Shea, and Kipp's "Jesuit Missions."

writer merit attention, although they came too late for incorporation in their proper place:

The mistletoe was dedicated to Mylitta, in whose worship every woman must once in her life submit to the sexual embrace of a stranger. When she concluded to perform this religious duty in honor of her acknowledged deity, she repaired to the temple and placed herself under the mistletoe, thus offering herself to the first stranger who solicited her favors. The modern modification of the ceremony is found in the practice among some people of hanging the mistletoe, at certain seasons of the year, in the parlor or over the door, when the woman entering that door, or found standing under the wreath, must kiss the first man who approaches her and solicits the privilege.—("Phallic Worship," Robert Allen Campbell, C. E., St. Louis, Mo., 1888, p. 202.)

Referring to previous remarks, on page 37, it may be noted that a curious instance of survival by contrariety is to be detected in what Picart relates of the Hebrew ceremonial of the present day. He says of the behavior of the Hebrew while praying, that he should carefully avoid gaping, spitting, blowing his nose, or emitting any exhalations:

Il doit éviter autant qu'il se peut de bailler, de cracher, de se moucher, de laisser aller des vents.—(Picart, Coutûmes et Cérémonies, &c., vol. 1, p. 126.)

All this information seems to be taken from the work of the Rabbi Leon of Modena.

In the above are seen the antipodes of the practices characteristic of the worship of Baal-Peor which the prophets had so much trouble in eradicating from the minds of the chosen people.

www.ingramcontent.com/pod-product-compliance
Lightning Source LLC
Chambersburg PA
CBHW021544270326
41930CB00008B/1350
9783337262709